A Guide to Common Plants of Lake Mead National Recreation Area

A GUIDE TO
COMMON PLANTS
of
LAKE MEAD
NATIONAL RECREATION AREA

Elizabeth A. Powell • Frederick H. Landau • Lawrence R. Walker

UNIVERSITY OF NEVADA PRESS | *Reno & Las Vegas*

University of Nevada Press | Reno, Nevada 89557 USA
www.unpress.nevada.edu
Copyright © 2023 by University of Nevada Press
Manufactured in the United States of America
FIRST PRINTING
Cover photographs © by Elizabeth A. Powell, Frederick H. Landau, and Lawrence R. Walker
Cover design by Diane MacIntosh

LIBRARY OF CONGRESS CATALOGING-IN-PUBLICATION DATA
Names: Powell, Elizabeth A. (Elizabeth Ann), 1949 author. | Landau, Frederick H., author. | Walker, Lawrence R.,
    author.
Title: *A guide to common plants of Lake Mead National Recreation Area* / Elizabeth A. Powell, Frederick H. Landau,
    Lawrence R. Walker.
Description: Reno ; Las Vegas : University of Nevada Press, [2022] | Includes bibliographical references and
    index. | Summary: "This book introduces the reader to the 183 most common plants of Lake Mead National
    Recreation Area, the sixth most visited park in the U.S., with 7.5 million visitors each year. It provides pictures
    and descriptions of each plant, and educates the reader about basic botany, plant life forms, and the different
    roles of native and non-native plants and their interactions with animals. This book will substantially enhance
    the desert experience for visitors."—Provided by publisher.
Identifiers: LCCN 2022038205 | ISBN 9781647790981 (paperback) | ISBN 9781647790998 (ebook)
Subjects: LCSH: Plants—Lake Mead National Recreation Area (Ariz. and Nev.)—Identification. | Botany—Lake
    Mead National Recreation Area (Ariz. and Nev.)—Handbooks, manuals, etc. | Plant ecology—Lake Mead
    National Recreation Area (Ariz. and Nev.)—Handbooks, manuals, etc. | Plants—Habitat—Lake Mead National
    Recreation Area (Ariz. and Nev.)—Handbooks, manuals, etc. | Lake Mead National Recreation Area (Ariz. and
    Nev.)
Classification: LCC QK142 .P69 2022 | DDC 582.1309793/12—dc23/eng/20220831 LC record available at https://
    lccn.loc.gov/2022038205

The paper used in this book meets the requirements of American National Standard for Information Sciences—
Permanence of Paper for Printed Library Materials, ansi/niso z39.48–1992 (R2002).

This book is dedicated to Patrick Leary
for his extensive explorations throughout
the Mojave Desert recording and collecting plants.
He is one who stoops, looks, lays on his belly with
camera in hand, and points out to others the
wonder of plant lives:

'Tis very pregnant,
The jewel that we find, we
stoop and take't
Because we see it; but
what we do not see
We tread upon, and never
think of it.

—William Shakespeare

Contents

Preface

We wrote this book to help the millions of annual visitors and local residents identify and enjoy the most common and conspicuous plants in Lake Mead National Recreation Area (LMNRA). Currently, there is no book-length guide to these plants. The entire flora of LMNRA contains about 1,000 plant species, but we have chosen the 183 plants that the reader is most likely to encounter, particularly around Lakes Mead and Mohave. Many plant species that we do not cover emerge only when conditions are particularly wet or only are found in remote areas of LMNRA. We use photos taken by the authors unless otherwise noted. We briefly introduce the region, basic plant ecology, and plant communities, then explain how we organize the plants by life form (tree, shrub, cactus, yucca, grass, aquatic, wildflower) and by flower color within the wildflowers. We provide a visual aid to plant structures in the back of the book.

We love the desert Southwest where we each have spent three or more decades researching, exploring, hiking, and botanizing. LMNRA, in particular, is spectacularly diverse in its geology, geography, biology, and human history, making it a wonderful place to explore. We hope that this book will enrich each reader's experience of the plants that they find in their rambles and adventures.

We gratefully acknowledge Paula Garrett for providing a map of LMNRA, in consultation with the National Park Service. Photographs, for the most part, were provided by the authors; photographs were also provided by Jim André, Pat Leary, and Kathlyn Powell. We also thank Cindy Phillips for her support of this project as well as Donald Davidson, Rosie Dempsey, and Maria Volborth, for their interest in the book's development. We are grateful to the School of Life Sciences, University of Nevada Las Vegas, for financial support.

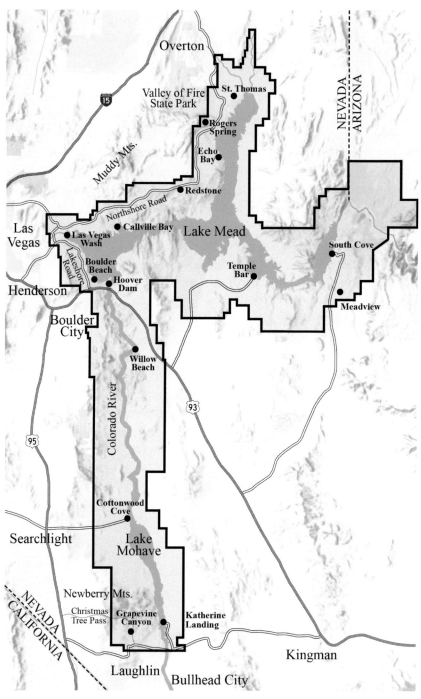

Map of Lake Mead National Recreation Area. The base map is from **ARCGIS** and uses sources from **BLM**, **CGIAR**, **EPA**, Esri, Garmin, **HERE**, **METI/NASA**, **NPS**, **SafeGraph**, and **USDA**.

Introduction

Lake Mead National Recreation Area (LMNRA) was created in 1964 and is the oldest and largest national recreation area in the country. LMNRA encompasses the country's largest reservoir (Lake Mead), as well as another large reservoir (Lake Mohave). The recreation area has a total land mass of 1.5 million acres (607,000 hectares) in Nevada and Arizona along 165 miles (265 kilometers) of the Colorado and Virgin River Basins. The total shoreline of both reservoirs is 790 miles (1,271 kilometers) when the reservoirs are full. Managed by the National Park Service, LMNRA attracts over 7.5 million people each year, making it the sixth most visited park in the United States, with visitors enjoying both water- and land-based recreation.

The diverse geology of the area reflects a complex, two-billion-year history of faulting, uplift, subduction, and erosion. Today, that history results in a delightful array of textures and colors produced by ancient seabeds, sand dunes, granite domes, volcanic ash, and lava. LMNRA, located in the eastern part of the Mojave Desert, receives an average of only 4 inches (100 millimeters) of rain per year, which results in minimal soil development. Two thirds of that rain arrives in gentle, winter rains that soak into the arid soils and help trigger germination of spring wildflowers. The other third arrives as sudden, often torrential summer storms that rapidly run off the land and reshape erosion channels.

Human history at LMNRA extends back at least ten thousand years, at a time when the climate was cooler and wetter, which resulted in an abundance of fish and large game animals. Petroglyphs hint at the lives of people who were finely attuned to their environment. Native people were adapted to the stable resources of the Colorado River, and developed different customs than those adapted to the more transient resources of the Mojave Desert. Southern Paiutes dominated the LMNRA region at the time of contact with people of European descent. Western migration of people of European descent occurred first by trails, then railroads and roads, particularly through the Virgin River Gorge (Old Spanish Trail) and the southernmost part of LMNRA (Mojave Trail, Route 66, and Southern Railroad). The landscape was further altered by mining, the construction of the Hoover Dam (1931–36) and Davis Dam (1942–52), and rapid urbanization in the Las Vegas Valley. Current land use policies in and around LMNRA regarding water rights, land rights-of-way, and recreation and conservation priorities were affected as well. The current, decades-long drought in the Colorado River Basin accentuates water management issues throughout the West and has led to drastically reduced water levels in Lake Mead.

View from Black Butte north to Fortification Hill across Lake Mead

LMNRA is so vast that it encompasses a wide range of habitats supporting several plant communities. Our focus in this book is to provide an easily accessible guide to the most common and conspicuous plants. We focus on plants found in the most visited sites (shorelines, campgrounds, popular trails, gathering places, and scenic highlights) that are either commonly found in abundance across large areas or conspicuously large or unusual, such as cacti and yuccas. We do not cover plants found only in the remote section of the park north of the Colorado River in Arizona, which is part of Grand Canyon-Parashant National Monument and jointly administered by the National Park Service and the Bureau of Land Management. The Grand Canyon-Parashant National Monument is largely a high-elevation plateau that is remote and has a flora that is mostly distinct from the lower elevations of LMNRA.

PLANT ECOLOGY

In this section, we briefly introduce a few basic principles about how plants interact with their environment to clarify the context in which plants of LMNRA grow. We discuss plant structure, seasonality and desert adaptations, plant-plant interactions (both positive and negative), and plant-animal interactions (pollination, dispersal, and herbivory).

Plant Structure

When you look at desert plants you might notice a few that are taller than you are. These are likely trees or yuccas (see section on life forms for details). Then your eye drops to plants that are about knee to shoulder height; these are mostly cacti and shrubs. Shrubs, the dominant life form in LMNRA, are woody and perennial (that is, plants that live for more than one growing season). As you study them, you will notice lots of different shapes, sizes, and colors. These clues help to identify them. Sedges and grasses, with their distinctive growth form, range in height, some growing as tall as shrubs. Aquatic plants are found in the shallow water near the shoreline of both lakes. Wildflowers are mostly herbaceous (not woody) and generally no taller than knee height. A subset of these are only about the height of your shoes and require bending over or even laying down on your belly to observe them closely, hence their nickname "belly plants." The majority of wildflowers are annuals, living only one year or season. They typically grow quickly, flower and set seed, all within a few months in spring or autumn.

The detailed structures of plants and their flowers are useful in identifying plants that, at first glance, look very similar. It helps to understand a few basics about how leaves are shaped and arranged on the stems, and how flowers are constructed and positioned on the inflorescence. In LMNRA, for example, there are many yellow sunflowers (or daisies). To properly identify them, one must learn a bit about the flower head. Each sunflower is really a combination of many flowers, both around the edge (ray flowers) and in the center (disk flowers). Although we do not go into great detail in this book, we do have some line drawings of plant structures and a glossary of critical terms at the back of the book. We also provide a section of suggested reading for further exploration of botanical details. Sometimes, when there are many related species, we present only one or two of the most common ones.

Seasonality and Desert Adaptations

Plants that thrive in LMNRA are adapted to long, hot summers, cool but not cold winters, and months or even years without rain. The perennial plants survive a lack of water during large portions of the year, blistering high heat, and potential sun damage. Local plants have evolved to address these challenges through various methods: Some plants have succulent tissues that hold water (cacti and yuccas); others are woody (trees and shrubs) and may drop their leaves during droughts. Leaves have tiny pores (stomata) that, when open for gas exchange needed for photosynthesis, also lose water. These pores may be sunken in the leaf surface or closed during the heat of the day to prevent water loss. Other plants have shiny or light-colored leaves that reflect sunlight. As you explore, you may notice that not many plants have very large leaves. Small leaves are a good adaptation to low water availability in the Mojave Desert. Drought-deciduous plants typically lose their leaves during the dry, hot, summer months, but are capable of quickly responding to warm-season rains by producing a burst of new foliage. Annual plants grow, flower, and set seed quickly when water is available, and survive as seeds during the long

Creosotebush in winter   Desert trumpet in winter

summer and fall droughts. The seeds then germinate when conditions are cool and wet during the period of the year when survival is likely to be guaranteed.

Desert plants are not always showy and colorful. In fact, much of the year, they may look leafless and dead. Many plants become invisible as seeds in the soil or die back to a perennial root. Similar to other plant guides, we mostly use pictures of plants with nice, green foliage and splashy flowers or obvious fruits. However, we do include some examples of what a few desert plants look like during winter (see also Dune primrose in the white and cream flowers section).

Plant-Plant Interactions

Plants interact with their neighbors in ways that are both positive and negative for their own growth and survival. An example of a positive interaction is when large, established shrubs provide shelter, shade, and even nutrients for younger establishing shrubs or wildflowers, earning the nickname "nurse plants." Plants can also negatively affect their neighbors when they compete for water, sunlight, and nutrients. Under certain conditions, such as prolonged drought, the benefit of nurse plants can be offset by competition for water. Nonnative plants (recent invaders of the Mojave Desert) can have negative effects on native plants in several ways. Certain nonnative grasses grow faster than native wildflowers in a wet spring, usurping water that the native plants could have used for germination and growth. When these grasses die, their dead leaves can promote fires that the nonnative grasses may survive, but many native plants do not. Nonnative Saltcedar shrubs can choke out native wetland plants by growing faster, surviving floods better, and by contaminating the soil with salt-laden leaves. Nonnative plants have been accidentally and intentionally introduced to LMNRA and can be localized in the landscape or become invasive (spread widely; see the human introductions section under plant communities). The result of the spread of nonnative species is a reduction in the diversity of native shrubs and wildflowers.

Plant-Animal Interactions

Many plants rely on animals for pollination or dispersal. Open sunflowers are available to most pollinating insects, while closed or narrowly tubular flowers may require pollinators to crawl inside the flower to reach nectar hidden at the base of petals. Some flowers require a pollinator, such as hummingbirds or some species of moths, to hover before the flower and to have a tongue long enough to reach inside the flower. Dispersal of plants by animals can occur when seeds stick to the fur of passing animals or when animals such as rodents bury or cache (hide) seeds. Another

Creosotebush with annuals

form of seed dispersal occurs when animals, such as birds, consume fruits and defecate seeds in other places. Finally, humans can also disperse seeds, either inadvertently or on purpose. For instance, humans introduced nonnative plants such as California fan palm for landscaping and some have spread to other areas of LMNRA.

Plants are most successful when their leaves and stems are not eaten by animals. Damage to plants by hungry animals (herbivory) can be deterred by spines and thorns. Other types of protection are conferred by woody tissues and resins that lack nutrients and reduce digestibility of leaves and stems, or by chemical irritants, such as bitter or toxic alkaloids that can discourage herbivory.

PLANT COMMUNITIES

LMNRA features a wide range of plant communities, determined by such variables as elevation, soil type, water availability, and human introductions, but these communities have considerable overlap. We name the first four communities after their respective dominant species.

Creosotebush

The Creosotebush community is the most common desert community within the LMNRA, especially on slopes (bajadas) between 1,000–3,500 feet (300–1,070 meters) elevation. Creosotebush is the most visually distinct plant but is often codominant with the more numerically abundant White bursage, which is a smaller, more compact shrub. Other plants commonly found in the Creosotebush community include Brittlebush, Shadscale, Desert holly, Nevada ephedra, and Pima rhatany.

Creosotebush community at Redstone   Blackbrush community at Christmas Tree Pass

Blackbrush

Blackbrush shrubs dominate this desert community at elevations between 3,200–5,400 feet (975–1645 meters), gradually overlapping with the Creosotebush community at its lower elevations. Blackbrush thrives in well-drained but shallow soils underlain by impermeable, calcium-rich caliche soils. At its lowest elevation, the Blackbrush community can reach the highest number of species of any Mojave Desert shrub community, sometimes with over 40 species of perennial plants. Other plants commonly associated with Blackbrush include Sticky snakeweed, Desert almond, Joshua tree, and Mojave yucca. At higher elevations, Blackbrush can form almost pure stands with few associated species. This community is most abundant in the Newberry Mountains and around the Meadview section of LMNRA.

Joshua Tree

The Joshua tree is an iconic plant of the Mojave Desert and distinguishes this community. The branches of this yucca often reach over 20 feet (6 meters) tall. The community has a broad elevational range (2,500–6,600 feet; 760–2,010 meters) but is most abundant from 3,100–5,500 feet (950–1675 meters). Joshua trees are uncommon in LMNRA except around Meadview. Blackbrush and Creosotebush are typical understory plants in this community. Both Joshua tree and Blackbrush communities are increasingly vulnerable to fires that are promoted by invasive grasses, public land grazing, and climate warming.

Pinyon Pine-Juniper

The Pinyon pine-Juniper (or "PJ") community is an open woodland vegetation that is typically found between 4,000–8,000 feet (1,220–2,440 meters) but can occur as low as 2,000 feet (610 meters) in the Newberry Mountains. In LMNRA, the dominant

Joshua tree community at Meadview   Pinyon pine–Juniper community at Christmas Tree Pass

species are California juniper and Singleleaf pinyon pine. These two trees can each grow as pure stands, but they often occur together. Typical understory species in the PJ community include Blackbrush, Banana yucca, Mojave yucca, and several species of cacti and grasses. These open woodlands, like others in the Southwest, are subject to fire, and when burned, can be replaced by understory shrubs and grasses. Regeneration of the Singleleaf pinyon pine is usually from seeds buried (cached) by Pinyon jays or rodents. Commercially available pine nuts harvested in the southwestern US usually come from Twoleaf pinyon pines that grow south of LMNRA.

Wetlands

In LMNRA, either continuously or intermittently available water supports plant communities in five types of habitats: aquatic, lakeshore, riverbank, spring, and alkali shrub. In the aquatic community, plants such as Spiny naiad and Fennel-leaf pondweed grow in the shallow waters of Lakes Mead and Mohave.

The lakeshores of Lakes Mead and Mohave vary in size depending on water levels in the two reservoirs. Those levels are determined by snowfall in the Rocky Mountains and subsequent drainage into the Colorado River and water releases from the reservoirs. Lake Mohave's shoreline remains relatively stable (within about 10 feet [3 meters] of full capacity at 647 feet [197.2 meters] above sea level), but, in late 2022, Lake Mead's shoreline was down 185 feet (56 meters) to 1044 feet (318 meters) from its full capacity at 1229 feet (375 m) above sea level. Because Lake Mead has not been at full capacity since 1983, various plant communities have established themselves in the once-flooded and now-dry drawdown zone. The initial shoreline and early drawdown levels support native Goodding's black willow and invasive Saltcedar shrubs, but as water levels drop, more drought-tolerant species such as Cheesebush and Lenscale invade the drawdown zone. Dense swards of invasive

Aquatic community at Crawdad Cove

Lakeshore community at Crawdad Cove

Mediterranean grass readily mark the drawdown zone, particularly as dry yellow stalks in winter.

In some riverbank communities, such as along the Las Vegas Wash, water is continuously available and supports stands of tall trees, including Fremont cottonwood and Goodding's black willow, sometimes referred to as "gallery forests." Dense shrub thickets of Arrowweed, Lenscale, or Saltcedar are often present. In dry washes (episodically inundated riverbeds), surface water is often absent, and plants have adapted by tapping the groundwater. Typical plants in dry washes include Desert willow, Catclaw, Western honey mesquite, Screwbean mesquite, Cheesebush, and Black-banded rabbitbrush.

Springs and associated marshes provide a perennial source of reliable water for Arrowweed, Common reed, and Southern cattail. Rogers Spring and Blue Point Spring are fed by groundwater that is pushed to the surface by fault lines deep below the soil surface. In the past, the surface waters were fringed with a well-developed ring of planted, nonnative California fan palms and Date palms. Nonnative Saltcedar and native Canyon grape, California sawgrass, and Southern cattail were also common. The California fan palms and Saltcedar have recently been removed from Rogers and Blue Point Springs to restore native vegetation to the springs. Springs at Grapevine Canyon in the Newberry Mountains as well as in Bridge Canyon, Sacaton Wash, and other areas scattered throughout LMNRA maintain native wetland vegetation that includes American bulrush, Saltgrass, and Alkali sacaton.

Alkali shrub vegetation is found at the interface between wetlands and the drier desert uplands where soils are salty due to high rates of evaporation of ground water. This vegetation can also be scattered within the other wetland communities where soil conditions are particularly salty, or on the edges of playas (dry lake beds) elsewhere in the Mojave Desert. Plants tolerant of these salty soils include Arrowweed, Shadscale, Desert holly, and Alkali sacaton. Western honey mesquite and

Riverbank community at Las Vegas Wash

Dry wash community at Pinto Valley

Spring community at Grapevine Canyon

Alkali shrub community on Northshore Road

Saltcedar can also survive where salinity is reduced by drainage. Good examples of alkali shrub vegetation can be found along Northshore Road near the LMNRA entrance station outside Overton and in areas around Rogers and Blue Point Springs.

Sand

There are several sand dunes, notably Sandy Cove near Callville Bay, north and south of Katherine Landing, and Sandy Point near South Cove, but also in smaller pockets throughout LMNRA. There are also numerous pockets of eroding sandstone in LMNRA, such as Bowl of Fire and Redstone. Several plant species are adapted to this unstable, low nutrient, and seemingly very dry and hot habitat, including herbs such as Dune primrose and Sand verbena and grasses such as Big galleta and

Sand community at Boxcar Cove

Sand community at Redstone

Ricegrass. Deep-rooted shrubs and trees, including Western honey mesquite, Catclaw, and Saltcedar can also tap water beneath the sand.

Gypsum

Gypsum community at Blue Point Spring

Gypsum outcrops are abundant both north and south of Lake Mead, particularly along Northshore Road from Bitter Springs Valley to Overton and north of the Temple Bar Road east of Bonelli Bay. This white mineral, composed of calcium sulfate, often forms lovely, translucent crystals, and is found both as small hills and in veins that form streaks in other rocks, such as sandstones and conglomerates. Many of the small, gypsum-covered hills were formed by deposits from now-dry springs. The plants that grow on gypsum outcrops have adapted to tolerate the unusual chemical composition of the soil better than most desert plants. Plants adapted to growing on gypsum include Thurber's sandpaper plant, Sunray, Las Vegas bearpoppy, and Palmer's phacelia.

Human Introductions

Humans have always moved plants around, for agricultural, horticultural, scientific, educational, and aesthetic purposes. This introduction of nonnative species often creates new communities. Intentional plantings in LMNRA occur around park buildings, campgrounds, picnic areas, and boat launches. Native plants that have been added to these public places include Desert willow, Western honey mesquite, Screwbean mesquite, Fremont cottonwood, Ocotillo, and various cacti. Nonnative introductions include three plants native to the Sonoran Desert (California fan

Human influences at Cottonwood Cove

Oleander shrub in campground on Lakeshore Road

Eucalyptus trees in campground at
Cottonwood Cove

Olive in campground at Las Vegas Wash

palm, Mexican fan palm, Paloverde) and plants native to other arid countries (Athel, Date palm, Eucalyptus, Oleander, Olive, and Saltcedar). Accidental introductions occur when seeds or plant parts of nonnative plants hitch rides in the water or on vehicle tires, hikers' socks, or in potted soil. Nonnative plants can also naturalize, which means to escape from landscape plantings and spread into favorable habitats within the desert. Plants that have naturalized to varying degrees in LMNRA include Paloverde, Athel, Saltcedar, Date palm, California fan palm, Mexican fan palm, Red brome, Cheatgrass, Mediterranean grass, Sahara mustard, and African mustard. Introduced plants that do not appear to spread from localized plantings

11

Fan palms at campground on Lakeshore Road

include species of Oleander, Eucalyptus, and Olive. The palms, commonly planted in camping areas, have spread from plantings, such as at Rogers Spring, but are now being removed by LMNRA.

LIFE FORMS

We have organized this book by life form as a useful first category for identification. As with any categorization, life form is somewhat arbitrary, so when in doubt, look in other likely categories for your plant. We explain below how to identify each life form.

Trees

We define trees as woody, perennial plants generally growing at least 6 feet (1.8 meters) tall and with a more-or-less defined central stem. Some of the plants found in the tree category also grow as shrubs. Note that we include Joshua tree within the yucca section.

Shrubs

We define shrubs as woody, perennial plants that are generally less than 6 feet tall and lacking a central stem. Under favorable growing conditions, shrubs such as Creosotebush can grow over 6 feet tall but retain their branched central stems.

Cacti

Cacti are succulent plants that are adapted to hot, dry desert environments in several ways. They store water in their fleshy tissues and usually protect this vital resource with spines that reduce water loss by reflecting light and shading the stem surface. Although most of our cacti lack proper leaves, their green stems allow them to photosynthesize. The surface pores (stomata) of cacti open only at night to take in carbon dioxide needed for photosynthesis. This timing allows cacti to limit water loss during the cooler nighttime temperatures. Cacti have many fine roots near the soil surface, an adaptation for water uptake after even light rains. These fine roots can grow within hours of a rainfall event and can be sloughed off during droughts. The ribbed stems of cacti enable them to expand to store water, then contract during droughts.

Yuccas

Yuccas, like cacti, are succulents. However, some yuccas open their pores during the daytime and some only at night, to reduce water loss. Yuccas have also adapted to potential water loss by having thick, leathery leaves and both shallow and deep roots, and by growing in generally cool, high elevation environments.

Sedges and Grasses

LMNRA has both perennial sedges and grasses and annual grasses. Sedges have solid, triangular stems in cross section and leaves spirally arranged in threes. Grasses have mostly hollow, round stems and alternating long, narrow leaves that wrap around the stem at their base, forming a sheath. Sedges and grasses in LMNRA range from Fluffgrass that is only several inches tall to Common reed that can grow over 10 feet (over 3 meters) tall.

Aquatic Plants

Aquatic plants rely on submersion in water and are most abundant in late summer in the comparatively warm, shallow edges of Lakes Mead and Mohave. They lack the rigid structures of terrestrial plants and will desiccate and die when blown or brought ashore.

Wildflowers

Our wildflower category, organized by flower color, is mostly nonwoody plants that are not grasses or grass-like. Annual plants complete their entire life cycle from seed to seed within one season or a few months. In LMNRA, there are spring annuals that germinate in early spring after wet winters and summer annuals that germinate in late summer after summer rains. Some plants placed in the wildflower category can live for two to three years or longer and have a semiwoody base. As with life forms, assigning wildflowers to a particular category can be imprecise.

Plant Descriptions

We organize the plant descriptions first by life form (trees, shrubs, cacti, yuccas, sedges and grasses, aquatic plants, wildflowers). We further divide the wildflowers by flower color (white and cream; yellow and orange; red, pink, and magenta; blue and purple; and inconspicuous. Within life form (and color for wildflowers), we organize the plants alphabetically by the Latin name for the plant family and then alphabetically by genus and species, so that closely related plants will be adjacent in the book. The common names are listed first but are not standardized. We chose the most appropriate common names for the LMNRA region and listed additional common names in parentheses. The scientific name, a two-part Latin name that is italicized, is placed under the common name. In contrast to common names, scientific names are standardized worldwide. However, scientific names can change based on new knowledge about the plants' taxonomic and evolutionary relationships. Our primary source for scientific plant names was Jepson-eFlora, the online version of *The Jepson Manual of the Vascular Plants of California*. We also consulted the second edition of *The Jepson Manual*, the *Flora of North America*, and the USDA Plant Database. Subspecies and varieties are noted only when necessary to distinguish a listed plant from a related one not covered in this book. Synonyms (alternate) scientific or family names are noted when recent name changes may cause confusion for the reader. In addition, the authors of each scientific name follow the names in the text and allow the reader to look up the original paper or book in which the plant has been described. At the end of the wildflower section, we provide a cross reference guide to other life forms with the same flower color, so the reader can find, for instance, yellow-flowered shrubs.

Trees

Trees are limited to areas with moist soils, such as near wetlands and in uplands, and provide welcome shade in the hot desert. Tree fruits provide valuable food for desert wildlife. We include several nonnative invasive trees here (Paloverde, Athel) and mention others in Human Introductions under Plant Communities.

DESERT WILLOW

Chilopsis linearis (Cav.) Sweet
subsp. *arcuata* (Fosberg)
Bignonia Family (Bignoniaceae)

Desert willow is a small tree that typically grows to 10- to 15-feet tall. It is generally found in lower elevation washes and along shorelines in LMNRA and has been planted extensively in camping and picnic areas. The flowering Desert willow is a lovely sight in the late spring and summer, with numerous, fragrant flowers streaked with pink and magenta that attract bees and hummingbirds. It is not a true willow but rather a relic of a geologic era when the climate was tropical. This tree resembles a true willow because of its elongated, drooping leaves. This species is the only native plant of the Bignonia (or Catalpa) family in Nevada, although other species in the family are widely planted and some have even naturalized. Desert willow is horticulturally important in the Southwest as a drought-tolerant landscape tree.

CALIFORNIA JUNIPER

Juniperus californica Carriere
Cypress Family (Cupressaceae)

The most likely place to find California juniper is in the Newberry Mountains near the height of Christmas Tree Pass. These trees are evergreen and can grow to 10 feet tall. California juniper is a gymnosperm and is dioecious: female trees produce small, seed-bearing cones that resemble fleshy berries, and male trees produce pollen-bearing cones. California juniper is associated with Singleleaf pinyon pine at higher elevations in the Newberry Mountains. Occasionally, you might see the parasitic Juniper mistletoe growing on the branches. The tree also supports a number of birds found along Christmas Tree Pass, such as Scott's oriole, Mourning dove, Lesser goldfinch, and Ladder-backed woodpecker.

PALOVERDE

Parkinsonia aculeata L.
Legume Family (Fabaceae)

In LMNRA, Paloverde was intentionally planted as a desert ornamental around buildings and in developed areas. A few individuals have escaped into the natural landscape, such as along the shoreline at Katherine Landing and along Lakeshore Road. Paloverde is a small, intricately branched thorny tree with smooth, green bark, which typically grows 15–20 feet tall. Flowers of Paloverde (April to May) are dark yellow with orange spots, and the uppermost petal turns red with age. Flowers are borne in clusters at the ends of branches. The tree may not flower in years of prolonged drought. In Spanish, *paloverde* means "green stick." *Parkinsonia* is named for John Parkinson (1567–1650), a London herbalist and botanist.

WESTERN HONEY MESQUITE

Prosopis glandulosa Torr. var.
torreyana (L. D. Benson)
Legume Family (Fabaceae)

Western honey mesquite typically grows along washes, in sandy valleys, and occasionally on sand dunes. The tree has long roots (up to 200 feet long) that allow Western honey mesquite to reach water sources, such as those deep under sand dunes. The inflorescence of Western honey mesquite is a dense spike of hundreds of yellow flowers, some of which develop into a straight, elongated pea-like pod. The leaves are pinnately compound and made up of many hairless, paired leaflets. Although this plant can grow to over 15 feet tall, in LMNRA it grows as low mounds in what appear to be dry washes in areas around Rogers Spring. It can also be seen in a few places along Northshore Road and in washes throughout LMNRA.

SCREWBEAN MESQUITE

Prosopis pubescens Benth.
Legume Family (Fabaceae)

Screwbean mesquite is a close relative of Western honey mesquite and similar in appearance, but it differs in some visible ways. Screwbean mesquite is generally a smaller tree (up to 10 feet tall) and has smaller, hairy leaflets. Its fruits are tightly coiled pods that grow in clusters at the end of branches. Although Screwbean mesquite also has deep roots, it is more restricted to sites near surface water or shallow groundwater. Where you see Screwbean mesquite in the landscape, you will also see water nearby, which is not necessarily the case with Western honey mesquite. Look for both species at Rogers Spring and in washes throughout LMNRA.

SMOKETREE

Psorothamnus spinosus (A. Gray) Barneby
Legume Family (Fabaceae)

One of the few locations for Smoketree within LMNRA is Nevada Telephone Cove on the southwestern shore of Lake Mohave. Smoketree is more common in the Sonoran and Colorado Deserts of California and Arizona. These few trees were used for firewood by campers in Telephone Cove for years, before the area was fenced off. Now camping is only allowed in areas where the tree mostly does not occur. The common name refers to the leafless, grayish, smoky appearance of the tree before it produces its indigo-blue clusters of pea-like flowers in late spring. The ends of branches are spine-tipped. Small leaves and leaflessness are common traits in desert plants. By minimizing a canopy of leaves, and carrying out photosynthesis through green stems, this 7- to 10-foot-tall tree can effectively minimize water loss and increase survivability in its arid environment.

CATCLAW

Senegalia greggii (A. Gray) Britton & Rose
Legume Family (Fabaceae)

Catclaw is a common shrub and sometimes a small tree in LMNRA. It is named for the curved prickles on stems that resemble the claw of a cat, which will definitely grab you if you come in contact with them. This plant was originally placed in the genus *Acacia,* but was recently moved to the genus *Senegalia,* as the prickles more resemble those of similar trees in Africa, Asia, and Australia. Flowers (April to June) are produced in dense, cylindrical spikes with many stamens but no petals. Each flower is cream-colored to yellow and is sweetly fragrant, which attracts butterflies and bees. The fruit is a twisted and flattened pea pod with hard, wax-covered seeds. Catclaw is found throughout LMNRA in washes and on roadsides. The tree is particularly obvious and large along Temple Bar Road and Detrital Wash, where the trees are the tallest (to 20 feet) in LMNRA. Catclaw also harbors Mistletoe, the berries of which are the favorite food of the state-protected Phainopepla birds. Phainopepla can be seen in the tops of Catclaw and Western honey mesquite when the mistletoe berries are ripe in late winter and early spring.

TURBINELLA OAK (SHRUB LIVE OAK)

Quercus turbinella Greene
Oak Family (Fagaceae)

Turbinella oak, typically less than 20 feet tall, is found in the Newberry Mountains in LMNRA, especially in the Christmas Tree Pass area. It is a monoecious tree, which means that the plant produces separate male and female flowers on the same plant. The flowers appear from April to June. The male inflorescence (cluster of flowers) may be noticeable because it is a catkin, a drooping spike of flowers. The female flowers become noticeable when they mature into acorns. Acorns mature by late summer or autumn and are eaten by deer and rabbits or cached by various rodents and birds.

SINGLELEAF PINYON PINE

Pinus monophylla Torr. & Frém.
Pine Family (Pinaceae)

Singleleaf pinyon pine is a dominant species of the Pinyon pine-Juniper community. In LMNRA, this tree grows only in the Newberry Mountains and can be seen at the highest point of Christmas Tree Pass. It is a medium-size tree, growing up to 15 feet tall. The needles are unique to pines, with each needle growly singly out of the stem. All other pines in our area have two or more needles in a bundle. Cones develop over a period of two years and bear edible seeds that are both eaten and cached by birds and rodents.

FREMONT COTTONWOOD

Populus fremontii S. Watson subsp. *fremontii*
Willow Family (Salicaceae)

Fremont cottonwood is one of the largest trees in LMNRA, growing 30–50 feet tall. The trunk is grayish and becomes deeply furrowed as it matures. The bright green leaves are heart-shaped or triangular with pointed tips; they turn bright yellow in autumn. Male and female flowers are produced in February to March on separate trees. Fremont cottonwood trees are good indicators that water is nearby. The trees are mostly limited to growing along riverbanks and floodplains. They have been planted in developed areas and in campgrounds and can be found in Las Vegas Wash and near Rogers Spring. John C. Frémont was an important mid-nineteenth century explorer of the Great Basin and Mojave Deserts. The name cottonwood comes from the cottony hairs on the seeds of trees that have only female flowers. The seeds develop in May to June and can create a blanket of white fluff on the ground when they are dispersed by the wind.

GOODDING'S BLACK WILLOW

Salix gooddingii C. R. Ball
Willow Family (Salicaceae)

Goodding's black willow, a 30- to 50-foot-tall riverbank (riparian) tree, growing along rivers, marshes, seepage areas, and washes. Look for it along Las Vegas Wash. It has a high flood tolerance and requires moist, sandy beds for seed germination. In favorable environments, it can form dense groves because it reproduces by vegetative sprouts, as well as by seed. It often occurs with Fremont cottonwood and shrubs such as Shadscale and Saltcedar. Goodding's black willow is a dioecious species, which means that it bears male and female flowers on separate trees. Female flowers (March to June) cluster in catkins, which develop into capsule fruits containing seeds with cottony hairs. All willows produce salicin, which can be converted to salicylic acid, the active ingredient in aspirin.

TREE TOBACCO

Nicotiana glauca Graham
Nightshade Family (Solanaceae)

Tree tobacco is a sometimes-branched, non-native small tree (15 to 20 feet tall) that was introduced to our area from South America. Its yellow flowers (March to August) have elongated tubes with short, flaring lobes at the top of the tube, much like a trumpet. The tree produces small brown seed capsules that are filled with hundreds of tiny seeds, which can spread easily in moist places. Tree tobacco contains anabasine, an alkaloid similar to nicotine that, when extracted, is used to make insecticides. *Nicotiana* refers to Jean Nicot, the sixteenth century French ambassador responsible for introducing smoking tobacco to France in 1560. In recent years, Tree tobacco has spread rapidly and is now abundant along Las Vegas Wash.

ATHEL

Tamarix aphylla (L.) H. Karst.
Tamarisk Family (Tamaricaceae)

Athel is a nonnative, introduced, fast-growing, drought- and salt-tolerant evergreen tree native to Africa and the Middle East. It has been planted in LMNRA as a shade tree in developed areas and campgrounds and can be found in many places throughout the Mojave Desert. Athel has spread along the shoreline of Lake Mead to other areas of LMNRA. It can grow up to 60 feet tall. The gray-green leaves are scale-like and tightly wrapped around the stem, giving the stems a jointed appearance. Flowers (April to November) are white to pink with five free petals and five stamens. Although Athel can reproduce by seed at LMNRA, as discovered by botanists, it also can propagate vegetatively from the root crowns or from roots. In recent years, there has been an attempt by LMNRA personnel to completely remove Athel. Athel has hybridized with the closely related Saltcedar, essentially creating a new species of plant that is more drought tolerant and evergreen than is the invasive Saltcedar.

Shrubs

Shrubs are a dominant life form in LMNRA. They come in all shapes, sizes, and flower color (see cross references from wildflower sections). The tallest, such as Seepwillow, Arrowweed, and Saltcedar, are generally associated with moist soils, although drought-adapted plants like Creosotebush can grow tall where there is sufficient moisture, including along roadsides, in desert washes, and on sand dunes.

RUSH MILKWEED

Asclepias subulata Decne.
Dogbane Family (Apocynaceae)

Rush milkweed bears small, opposite leaves, especially after a rain, but the stems appear leafless throughout most of the year. An intriguing flat-topped cluster of cream to whitish-green flowers (April to December) bloom at the top of the rush-like stems. The fruit is a pod that bears seeds with long, silken hairs that may help the seeds disperse in the wind. Rush milkweed is an important larval host plant for the caterpillars of the Monarch butterfly. The caterpillars ingest the toxic sap and store the compounds in their bodies. These stored compounds deter predation of the caterpillars by birds.

WHITE BURSAGE (BURROBUSH)

Ambrosia dumosa (A. Gray) W. W. Payne
Sunflower Family (Asteraceae)

Sometimes the most ubiquitous plant is not the most conspicuous. White bursage is a codominant shrub with Creosotebush in the Creosotebush community. But whereas Creosotebush is visually dominant, White bursage is generally more numerous. It is a low, compact shrub that acts as a nurse plant, providing cover for many desert seedlings that would otherwise be exposed to harsh environmental conditions and herbivores. Like many other Mojave Desert shrubs, White bursage is drought-deciduous, dropping its leaves during periods of drought to prevent water loss. This shrub flowers in spring and can flower again in the fall, if there has been adequate summer rain. The flowers are small and greenish in color. Look for the fruit that develops into a spiny, purple-brown bur, suitable for catching onto the fur or feathers of passing animals.

WOOLLY BURSAGE

Ambrosia eriocentra (A. Gray) W. W. Payne
Sunflower Family (Asteraceae)

Plants in the genus *Ambrosia* are often called ragweeds or bursages. LMNRA has four species of *Ambrosia;* we cover three of them in this book. Woolly bursage flowers are inconspicuous because they lack showy petals and are wind pollinated. The copious pollen that they produce can contribute to seasonal allergies for many people. The fruits are burs that have radiating spines in a star-like pattern. Look for this plant in desert washes and sandy, alkaline soils, particularly in Grapevine Canyon, where large individuals can be found, often surrounded by water-driven debris in the broad sandy wash.

CHEESEBUSH

Ambrosia salsola (Torr. & A. Gray)
Strother & B. G. Baldwin
Sunflower Family (Asteraceae)

If you rub your hand along the green, photosynthetic stems of this nearly leafless shrub you will understand why it is called Cheesebush: it emits an odor that is very reminiscent of fragrant cheese or worn gym socks. Like all members of the *Ambrosia* genus, Cheesebush has separate male and female flowers borne on the same plant. The female flowers are noticeable because they are each surrounded by a shiny, papery, wing. Cheesebush is widely distributed throughout LMNRA, especially in sandy-gravelly desert washes and in disturbed areas. Some large stands occur in the drawdown zone of Boulder Basin, including at Boulder Beach and along Lakeshore Road.

CHAFFBUSH

Amphipappus fremontii Torr. & A. Gray
Sunflower Family (Asteraceae)

The species epithet, *fremontii,* is used for several plants in the southwestern US deserts and refers to John C. Frémont, an explorer, soldier, mapmaker, governor, US Senator, and presidential aspirant. The heads of the yellow, mostly disk flowers cluster together at the ends of flowering stems. Look for these plants in flower at Redstone in spring and early summer.

SEEPWILLOW (MULEFAT)

Baccharis salicifolia (Ruiz & Pav.) Pers.
Sunflower Family (Asteraceae)

The names of this upright shrub, Seepwillow and *Baccharis salicifolia,* both refer to the plant's resemblance to the leaves and riverbank habitats of true willows (*Salix* spp. in the Willow family). However, leaves of Seepwillow can be distinguished from true willows by the three prominent, vertical veins on the leaf blade; there is only one main vein on the leaves of true willows. This shrub has female flowers (*left*) and male flowers (*right*). Both true willows and Seepwillows grow in wetland areas within LMNRA, and both are capable of forming dense thickets. The name Mulefat comes from the old gold mining days when prospectors and cowboys would tie up their mules to the shrub for security and browse. Look for plants along the Colorado River at Pearce Ferry.

BROOM BACCHARIS

Baccharis sarothroides A. Gray
Sunflower Family (Asteraceae)

There are four species of *Baccharis* in LMNRA, some more common than others, but all are associated with moist environments such as riverbanks, wetlands, and washes. Broom baccharis is distinguished from Seepwillow by its vertical, broom-like stems and small, rounded leaves. The leaves generally drop by the time the flowers appear. Broom baccharis flowers later than Seepwillow, often in late spring and into the summer months. The clusters of flowers are notable by their glistening appearance, as if they were encased in clear amber. The glistening is due to the drying resins that surround the flower bracts (phyllaries). Look for this plant along the banks of Las Vegas Wash.

PARISH'S GOLDENEYE

Bahiopsis parishii (Greene)
E. E. Schill. & Panero
Sunflower Family (Asteraceae)

Initially inconspicuous, Parish's goldeneye becomes distinctive upon close examination. Its dark-green, triangular-shaped leaves are deeply pleated and are arranged opposite each other along the stem. The eight to fifteen yellow ray flowers are also pleated along their length. The shrub produces flowers in the spring months and, in the event of sufficient summer rains, can flower again in the early autumn months. This plant can be easily confused with Virgin River encelia, but the number of ray flowers is fewer and petals are generally not toothed in Parish's goldeneye. Look for this plant in the Creosotebush community along dry rocky slopes and in broad washes.

SWEETBUSH
(CHUCKWALLA'S DELIGHT)

Bebbia juncea (Benth.) Greene
var. *aspera* Greene
Sunflower Family (Asteraceae)

Sweetbush refers to this rounded shrub's aromatic fragrance, and Chuckwalla's delight refers to the Chuckwalla lizard that relishes this plant for food and cover. *Bebbia* is named in honor of Michael Bebb, a nineteenth-century botanist, and *juncea* refers to the rush-like or leafless stems. At first glance, the shrub can look like an unimpressive tangle of dry stems, but if you look closely at its flowers in spring you will see that they are clusters of yellow-orange, tubular disk flowers. Sweetbush is common along roadsides and in washes and rocky hillsides in the Creosotebush community throughout LMNRA.

BRITTLEBUSH
(INCIENSO)

Encelia farinosa Torr.
Sunflower Family (Asteraceae)

Brittlebush provides one of the earliest of the spectacular flower displays of the year in LMNRA. This common, rounded shrub has large, silvery-gray leaves in a dense ball topped by yellow sunflowers held 6 to 12 inches above leafless stalks. The central disk flowers of this shrub can be orange or reddish brown. The name Brittlebush refers to the shrub's brittle, easy-to-break stems. The Spanish name, Incienso, refers to the fragrance emitted when the dried sap was ritually burned in the early Spanish missions as incense. Masses of these shrubs in flower can be seen along both Lakeshore and Northshore Roads in March, as well as in washes and along roadsides throughout LMNRA.

VIRGIN RIVER BRITTLEBUSH

Encelia virginensis A. Nelson
Sunflower Family (Asteraceae)

Virgin River brittlebush is named for the Virgin River that drains into Lake Mead and merges with the Colorado River. The shrub is found along the river from southern Utah and throughout the LMNRA in the Creosotebush, Blackbrush, and Joshua Tree communities. Virgin River brittlebush is easily distinguished from Brittlebush by its smaller, greener leaves and white stems covered with short stiff hairs. The flower heads appear above the canopy of leaves throughout the spring months. The ray flowers have petals that are toothed. Virgin River brittlebush is an important food source for the Desert tortoise, especially in periods of low moisture availability. It is often an early pioneer in the plant community after a disturbance, such as fire, and is used to revegetate disturbed areas.

BLACK-BANDED RABBITBRUSH (MOJAVE RABBITBRUSH)

Ericameria paniculata (A. Gray) Rydb.
Sunflower Family (Asteraceae)

Black-banded rabbitbrush is often found growing in broad, dry washes. The stems of this 5-foot-tall shrub are dotted with resin glands, imparting a turpentine-like aroma when scratched or crushed. Black-banded rabbitbrush refers to the bands along its stems caused by a smut fungus. The flower heads are composed of about eight tubular disk flowers. There are no ray flowers. As the flowers mature, the seeds are topped with long, silky hairs (pappus), enabling seed dispersal by wind. Look for Black-banded rabbitbrush in large washes such as Callville Wash and Boxcar Cove.

STICKY SNAKEWEED

Gutierrezia microcephala (DC.) A. Gray
Sunflower Family (Asteraceae)

Sticky snakeweed is a much-branched small shrub that has dark-green, thread-like leaves and is distributed widely throughout LMNRA. The small, yellow flower heads glisten with resins and are comprised of small clusters of both ray and disk flowers. *Microcephala* refers to the small flower heads, which appear in late summer and early autumn. Although Sticky snakeweed is fire-intolerant, its many seeds remain viable in the soil and can quickly recolonize after burns or other disturbances. Look for this plant at Redstone and along Northshore Road.

ALKALI GOLDENBUSH

Isocoma acradenia (Greene) Greene
Sunflower Family (Asteraceae)

Alkali goldenbush is a rounded, resinous shrub that is found in sandy, alkali, or gypsum soils throughout LMNRA. It is noticeable by its white stems and spoon-shaped leaves. Its flower heads are composed of disk flowers only. Just below the yellow flowers you can see the vertically ranked bracts (phyllaries) that are green, rounded, and swollen, with a green resin gland at the top, appearing wart-like. Look for this shrub around Rogers Spring.

PYGMY CEDAR

Peucephyllum schottii A. Gray
Sunflower Family (Asteraceae)

Look for this large, dark-green shrub on hillsides in the lower elevations near Lake Mead and sometimes jutting out of rocky cliff faces. The cliff face may seem an inhospitable location for Pygmy cedar to take root, but the shade and overhanging rock helps to reduce water loss, and the crevices provide conduits for runoff water and root growth. Leaves of Pygmy cedar are like needles: short, linear, and covered with a sheen of resin that imparts a distinctive fragrance. *Peucephyllum* is a Greek word that refers to its pine- or fir-like leaves. The heads of disk flowers appear in March, are lemon-yellow, and sometimes fade to red as the flowers age. You can find this shrub in many places in LMNRA in the Creosotebush community.

ARROWLEAF

Pleurocoronis pluriseta (A. Gray)
R. M. King & H. Rob.
Sunflower Family (Asteraceae)

This unassuming shrub is easily identifiable by its unusual leaf shape. The small, arrow-shaped leaf blade is held aloft by a slender and elongated leaf stalk. The flower heads, which appear in spring, are comprised of pinkish-white disk flowers. Look for this plant in canyons and washes at lower elevations in LMNRA and also on cliff faces near damp habitats, including at Redstone and along the Historic Railroad Trail.

ARROWWEED

Pluchea sericea (Nutt.) Coville
Sunflower Family (Asteraceae)

Arrowweed is one of the most beautiful native plants in water edge habitats. It is a tall, upright shrub with straight branches. Underground stems (rhizomes) allow the shrub to grow into very dense thickets. The lance-shaped leaves are covered with silky white hairs and are uniformly crowded along the stem. Arrowweed displays a dense profusion of pink to rose-colored flowers at the top of its long stems in spring. It has been used for many purposes by Native Americans, but as its name implies, one of those uses was as arrow shafts. Look for this plant in abundance around Rogers Spring, in Las Vegas Wash, and on the shores of Lakes Mead and Mohave.

PAPERFLOWER
(PAPER-DAISY)

Psilostrophe cooperi (A. Gray) Greene
Sunflower Family (Asteraceae)

Paperflower is a white-stemmed shrub with linear leaves and clusters of yellow flowers in spring months. Each flower cluster is borne singly atop the stem. The rounded ray flowers have distinct notches at their tips, reflex backward toward the receptacle as they mature, and remain on the receptacle even after they dry to a papery thin, tan-colored petal. This plant is very attractive to hummingbirds, butterflies, and bees.

MOJAVE COTTONTHORN (HORSETHORN)

Tetradymia stenolepis Greene
Sunflower Family (Asteraceae)

Mojave cottonthorn is a medium-sized shrub found in the Creosotebush and Blackbrush communities along Christmas Tree Pass. The branches look white from their covering of dense hairs and are amply protected by long thick spines. Apparently, members of local Mojave tribes used the Mojave cottonthorn spines as needles for tattooing. Flower heads appear in spring months as neat bundles of light yellow disk flowers that elegantly rise just above the surrounding white cottony bracts. Flower photo by Jim André.

SPINY GOLDENBUSH

Xanthisma spinulosum (Pursh) D. R. Morgan & R. L. Hartm. var. *gooddingii* (A. Nelson) D. R. Morgan & R. I. Hartm.
Sunflower Family (Asteraceae)

Spiny goldenbush has wand-like, upright stems. The inflorescence is composed of yellow disk flowers in a tight cluster, surrounded by numerous ray flowers. *Xanthisma* refers to its yellow color, and *spinulosum* refers to the small spines along the lobed leaf edges. Spiny goldenbush grows in rocky areas and mountain slopes and is particularly noticeable in LMNRA at Redstone.

DESERT ALYSSUM	FOUR-WING SALTBUSH
Lepidium fremontii S. Watson	*Atriplex canescens* (Pursh) Nutt.
Mustard Family (Brassicaceae)	Goosefoot Family (Chenopodiaceae)

Desert alyssum is the only woody shrub in the Mustard family in Nevada. It can appear an unremarkable plant when not in flower but it becomes more noticeable from March to June when a profusion of small white flowers adorns the tops of branches. Flowers and fruit often intermix in the display, so look closely at the fruit and you will see a flat, round pod with a small notch at its apex. The leaves and fruits have a sharp, peppery fragrance and flavor. You can typically find this plant on or near gypsum soils.

The dry fruit of Four-wing saltbush encloses the seed within four papery wings, giving rise to its name. This is one of five native shrubs of the *Atriplex* genus found in LMNRA. Like its relatives, this shrub can tolerate high heat and low moisture availability and can grow in places with relatively high soil salinity. Leaves and stems have a greenish-gray appearance due to dense white hairs and are covered with salt crystals that are extruded by the leaves. The hairs reflect much of the incoming sunlight, which can reduce leaf surface temperatures. Most of these shrubs have male and female flowers borne on separate individuals. This shrub flowers in late spring and summer in LMNRA.

SHADSCALE

Atriplex confertifolia (Torr. & Frém.) S. Watson
Goosefoot Family (Chenopodiaceae)

Shadscale can be found in alkali flats, where it is adapted to saltier soils than most other plants. It is a widespread species that occurs in most of the western states. Shadscale is dioecious, so a single plant produces only male or female flowers. The flowers are small and sometimes reddish in color. Leaves are usually round and covered with dense gray scales. The fruits have two large bracts that come together like praying hands. Look for this shrub near Rogers and Blue Point Springs.

DESERT HOLLY

Atriplex hymenelytra (Torr.) S. Watson
Goosefoot Family (Chenopodiaceae)

Early in the year, when temperatures are low and moisture available, Desert holly is covered with green leaves. As conditions become warmer and drier, white hairs accumulate salt, which may deflect sunlight. Desert holly cuts a striking appearance in the landscape with its toothed, white, powdery leaves and reddish clusters of young flowers, giving it a passing resemblance to the unrelated European holly. This shrub flowers from late winter to spring and fruits are enclosed within two leaf-like bracts, as if cupped within a pair of praying hands. Desert holly grows mostly in saline and alkaline areas in Creosotebush and Alkali shrub communities.

LENSCALE
(QUAILBUSH, BIG SALTBUSH)

Atriplex lentiformis (Torr.) S. Watson
Goosefoot Family (Chenopodiaceae)

Lenscale is the largest of the saltbushes growing in LMNRA: It can grow to up to 8 feet tall. Like the other saltbushes, flowers are wind pollinated and the seeds are dispersed by wind, water, and some vertebrates, including Gambel's quail, which also uses the shrub's dense canopy for protection. Lenscale grows in saline and nonsaline soils and is often associated with water-edge habitats within LMNRA, along with Arrowweed, Western honey mesquite, Saltcedar, and other saltbushes. A distinguishing feature of Lenscale, separating it from the other LMNRA saltbushes, is its large size and triangular-shaped leaves. Lenscale is abundant along Las Vegas Wash.

WINTERFAT

Krascheninnikovia lanata (Pursh)
A. Meeuse & A. Smit
Goosefoot Family (Chenopodiaceae)

The common name, Winterfat, refers to the role of this plant as important winter forage for wildlife and domestic animals. Thick hairs on the leaves and stems make the shrub appear white. Male and female flowers of Winterfat appear in the spring months and grow in separate inflorescences on the same plant. Flowers are produced at the top of branches. This plant is found in higher elevations of LMNRA such as along Christmas Tree Pass. Stepan Krascheninnikov was a Russian botanist and explorer of Siberia and Kamchatka in the mid-1700s.

NEVADA EPHEDRA

Ephedra nevadensis S. Watson
Ephedra or Joint-fir Family (Ephedraceae)

This broom-like shrub, with jointed, furrowed, evergreen stems, is more closely related to pines and junipers than to flowering plants. Ephedras do not have proper flowers but bear their pollen (*right* male) and seeds (*left* female) in cones. The cones can have papery bracts and are light-colored, giving the overall appearance of a flower. There are six recorded species of *Ephedra* in LMNRA. Nevada ephedra has grayish-green stems that may be erect to spreading, and two scale-like, deciduous leaves that are opposite each other at each node on the stem.

TORREY EPHEDRA

Ephedra torreyana S. Watson
Ephedra or Joint-fir Family (Ephedraceae)

This ephedra can be distinguished from Nevada ephedra by its grey, fissured bark and grey and grooved stems. At each stem node there are three tiny leaves, distinguishing it from the two leaves on Nevada ephedra. This shrub occurs mostly in Gypsum communities in LMNRA. The stems branch at a wide angle, making the plant appear rangy and unkempt. This shrub is dioecious, meaning that each plant only produces male or female cones. The female plants produce cones that have numerous yellow bracts and make the plants superficially appear to be in flower.

SAND CROTON

Croton californicus Muell. Arg.
Spurge Family (Euphorbiaceae)

Sand croton is mostly found in sandy soils, dunes, and sandy washes. Look for it in dune communities in LMNRA, such as around South Cove in the Meadview Section of LMNRA and around Katherine Landing. Sand croton is a perennial herb or subshrub identifiable by its habitat, gray-greenish color, opposite leaves, and covering of star-shaped clusters of hairs. Female (*left*) and male (*right*) flowers are borne on separate plants. The fruit of a female Sand croton is a round, three-lobed capsule also covered by star-shaped clusters of hairs.

BUSH TREFOIL

Acmispon rigidus (Benth) Brouillet
Legume Family (Fabaceae)

Bush trefoil roots form nodules that contain nitrogen-fixing bacteria (*Rhizobium* spp.). The bacteria convert atmospheric nitrogen gas into a form that is usable by plants. This trait is important in soils where nitrogen sources are limited and is common in plants in the Legume family. Bush trefoil has erect, rigid stems. The 3 to 5 leaflets that make up the leaf can be arranged either opposite each other, or, more likely, radiate from a central point. The pea-like yellow flowers fade and become reddish with age. Look for this plant on slopes and in washes along Christmas Tree Pass.

INDIGOBUSH (FREMONT'S DALEA)

Psorothamnus fremontii (A. Gray) Barneby
Legume Family (Fabaceae)

For much of the year, Indigobush disappears into the background of the desert plains and dunes of the Creosotebush community. However, in spring, this medium-sized, spreading shrub lives up to its name with a canopy of numerous rich, deep blue, pea-like flowers. The blue flowers make a striking contrast with the sparse covering of green-silvery leaves and twisting grey-white stems of the shrub. The flowers are rarely seen in years of very little rainfall. You can find this shrub in the Creosotebush and Gypsum communities.

SPINY SENNA

Senna armata (S. Watson)
H. S. Irwin & Barneby
Legume Family (Fabaceae)

Just when you think the spring blooming period is over, Spiny senna comes into flower and becomes a ball of yellow on gravelly hillsides of the Creosotebush community. Spiny senna has mostly hairless, gray-green, and grooved branches. When its pinnately compound leaves drop, they leave a thick mid-vein that elongates into a weak spine. The bright yellow flowers are bilaterally symmetrical and not the pea-like flower that is usual for this family. Both the common and scientific name allude to the presence of spines.

OCOTILLO

Fouquieria splendens Engelm.
subsp. *splendens*
Ocotillo Family (Fouquieriaceae)

Ocotillo is not a cactus but superficially resembles one. It is a semisucculent spiny shrub with slender cane-like stems that grow from a short trunk up to 20 feet tall. After rain, leaves grow from the stems but wither and drop during hot, dry periods. Dense clusters of bright red tubular flowers appear at the end of the stems in the spring months. Ocotillo is abundant in the Sonoran Desert but grows in remote areas of the Arizona side of LMNRA, and you can find them planted at the Visitor Center, Temple Bar, and Echo Bay. Hummingbirds visit this plant when it is in flower.

PIMA RHATANY

Krameria erecta Schult.
Rhatany Family (Krameriaceae)

Like so many plants in hot, arid landscapes, Pima rhatany can be easily overlooked until it comes into flower. This dark, low-lying shrub produces spring flowers that are bright magenta and bilaterally symmetrical in shape with three upper and two lower petals. Its round fruit has many red spines. Like most desert plants, Pima rhatany has evolved water-conserving or water-gathering attributes, and the shrub has an additional strategy: the roots can graft to nearby plants in a semiparasitic relationship and steal water and nutrients. Look for this shrub anywhere in the Creosotebush community where it is often the third most common shrub after Creosotebush and White bursage in undisturbed habitats. Flower photo by Kathlyn Powell.

DESERT LAVENDER

Condea emoryi (Torr.) Harley &
J. F. Pastore
(*Hyptis emoryi* Torr.)
Mint Family (Lamiaceae)

This aromatic shrub grows in the more southern areas of LMNRA, particularly on the Arizona side of Lake Mohave in washes and along Fisherman's Trail near Katherine Landing. Desert lavender usually appears as a tall, grey-green, straggly shrub with triangular, woolly leaves. Small, violet, or light blue flowers grow in the axils of leaves. The flowers are very attractive to honeybees as a source of nectar.

DESERT SAGE

Salvia dorrii (Kellogg) Abrams
Mint Family (Lamiaceae)

When crushed, Desert sage leaves emit an intensely aromatic fragrance. The spring flowers are bilaterally symmetrical, or two-lipped, and come in variable shades of blue emerging from ruffles of pink bracts. The bottom lobes of the petals form a landing platform for bees and other pollinating insects. A close relative, Mohave sage (*Salvia mohavensis*) is found in LMNRA on canyon walls and steep rocky areas. The Mohave sage has flowers that have a lighter blue color than Desert sage. *Salvia* comes from Latin *servare* (to save) and refers to the medicinal properties of some members of the genus.

BLADDERSAGE

Scutellaria mexicana (Torr.) A. J. Paton
Mint Family (Lamiaceae)

Bladdersage is often associated with the sandy to gravelly soils of desert washes where it is readily discernible by its pattern of right-angled stems. Its leaves are small and opposite one another, and drop away under dry conditions. In spring months, Bladdersage produces white and violet two-lipped (pea-shaped) flowers. As the flowers grow, the rose-colored sepals become inflated and papery and enclose the four developing nutlets within, giving the impression of an inflated bladder or paper bag.

THURBER'S SANDPAPER PLANT

Petalonyx thurberi A. Gray
Stickleaf Family (Loasaceae)

Thurber's sandpaper plant is named for the stiff, abrasive recurved hairs on its leaves and stems. The leaves are triangular or roundish with blades that partially surround the stem; the leaves are smaller toward the tip of the stem. The white flowers have stamens that stick out beyond the petals. Thurber's sandpaper plant grows on gypsum soils within LMNRA along with Las Vegas bearpoppy and Palmer's phacelia. Look for this shrub along Northshore Road between Echo Bay and Overton Beach, and along Road 109 to St. Thomas.

GLOBEMALLOW
(DESERT MALLOW)

Sphaeralcea ambigua A. Gray
Mallow Family (Malvaceae)

Globemallow is one of the most common and conspicuous perennial shrubs of LMNRA in good flowering years. It produces a profusion of apricot-orange flowers from March to May. Each flower has five petals with one to many flowers clustering along the upper stems. Leaves have fine hairs that radiate from center spots like the rays of stars but can be irritating to sensitive skin. Look for this plant along roadsides, on the edges of washes, and along the Historic Railroad Trail.

DESERT BUCKWHEAT
(CALIFORNIA BUCKWHEAT)

Eriogonum fasciculatum Benth.
Buckwheat Family (Polygonaceae)

Desert buckwheat is a variably shaped shrub that has leathery leaves with curled edges. The white to pinkish flowers, although individually small, cluster together in a series of umbels above leafless stalks. Look for this common plant along Christmas Tree Pass and in rocky areas.

BLACKBRUSH	DESERT ALMOND
Coleogyne ramosissima Torr.	*Prunus fasciculata* (Torr.) A. Gray
Rose Family (Rosaceae)	Rose Family (Rosaceae)

Blackbrush can grow so densely in places in the Newberry Mountains and in the Meadview area of LMNRA that it forms its own community. Blackbrush has opposite clusters of leaves. It technically has no petals but four yellow sepals that are very petal-like. The grayish-green stems can darken after a rain, making the shrub look almost black. After a fire, Blackbrush does not resprout or seed readily and is typically replaced in the landscape by other species of plants. In the absence of fire or other major disturbance, the shrub reproduces with the aid of rodents that gather and cache the seeds.

Sometimes a plant may become noticeable because of organisms other than the plant itself. In spring, Desert almond often has the webbed pockets of Tent caterpillar moths (*Malacosoma californicum*) on its branches. The caterpillars gather inside the web during the day and forage outside the tent at night, feeding on the small, clustered leaves. The caterpillars eventually metamorphose into brown moths at maturity. Desert almond is a much-branched, 3- to 7-foot-tall shrub with spiny branch tips. It produces small, white flowers in spring, and small, green, almond-like fruits. Seeds within the fruit contain high levels of cyanide, making them very bitter and inedible. Look for Desert almond on dry hillsides and washes in Christmas Tree Pass area.

DESERT RUE
(TURPENTINE BROOM)

Thamnosma montana Torr. & Frém.
Rue Family (Rutaceae)

Desert rue is the only plant in the Rue or Citrus family that is native to Nevada and the Mojave Desert. Turpentine broom refers to its mostly leafless, broom-like, yellow-green stems. The stems are dotted with glands that resemble the glands on citrus rinds. If you rub or scratch the stems, the activated oils will impart a deeply pungent, citrus-like fragrance. *Thamnosma* is from Greek, meaning odorous shrub. The flowers bloom in spring and are deep-purple and tubular. The fruits are two-lobed, yellow-green, gland-dotted, and may look like miniature grapefruits. Look for this shrub in rocky places along Christmas Tree Pass.

BOX-THORN
(WOLFBERRY)

Lycium andersonii A. Gray
Nightshade Family (Solanaceae)

Box-thorn is an upright shrub with thorn-tipped, spreading, whitish branches that grows 3 to 5 feet tall. Leaves are small, slightly succulent, and are dropped during the hot, dry months. White to pale purple tubular flowers appear in spring months. Fruits are conspicuous many-seeded red berries, which may have been a source of food for Southern Paiutes. Box-thorn is rarely dominant in the local flora but is often interspersed with other shrubs in the Creosotebush and Blackbrush communities.

SALTCEDAR

Tamarix ramosissima Ledeb.
Tamarisk Family (Tamaricaceae)

Unfortunately, one of the most common plants along the shoreline and in the drawdown zone of Lake Mead is this nonnative invasive shrub from the Middle East and Africa. Salt-cedar refers to the plant's ability to tolerate salty water or soil by storing salt in specialized glands in its leaves. Eventually the leaves drop to the ground and make the soil too salty for many native plants. In addition to lake shore-lines, look for Saltcedar in moist, alkaline areas of LMNRA, especially washes and streambanks. Saltcedar was originally introduced to control erosion but has become a noxious species. Pink clusters of flowers are borne at the end of the branches from April to August. A mature Salt-cedar can produce over 500,000 seeds each year.

CANYON GRAPE (ARIZONA GRAPE)

Vitis arizonica Engelm.
Grape Family (Vitaceae)

Canyon grape is a woody deciduous vine with shredding bark and woolly stems, and grows in canyons and along rivers. The stems sprawl more than climb and can reach 20 feet in length. The leaves are heart-shaped and toothed, with tendrils developing opposite the leaves. Flowers emerge in spring opposite the leaves and are white or greenish, somewhat fragrant, and produce the edible (but some-times bitter), juicy, purplish-black berry fruit. In LMNRA, do not be surprised if the edible ber-ries of this vine are hard to find; birds and mam-mals eat the berries quickly when they begin to ripen. Look for Canyon grape in Grapevine Canyon and around Rogers Spring.

CREOSOTEBUSH

Larrea tridentata (DC.) Coville
Caltrop Family (Zygophyllaceae)

Anywhere you look in LMNRA you are likely to see Creosotebush, the most common and obvious shrub in the park. It is also a remarkable desert survivor. Creosotebush arrived in the Mojave Desert about 12,000 years ago and is now present throughout the North American deserts. Some plants have been dated to over 10,000 years old. Volatile resins on the leaves emit a distinctive fragrance to the air after rains. Many insects, including 22 species of bees, have coevolved with Creosotebush, using it as food or shelter. Some of these insects mimic the plant's leaf and stem coloration or its fuzzy seed pods to avoid being eaten by other animals.

Cacti

In this section we present twelve of the nineteen cacti species found in LMNRA. This remarkably hardy group of plants offer a delightful late-spring array of colored flowers that perhaps make it worth the challenge of avoiding their spines. The tallest cacti can reach over 6 feet tall and include Buckhorn cholla, Teddybear cholla, and Silver cholla. Diamond cholla and Barrel cactus can be up to 3 to 4 feet tall. The remainder of the cacti are generally shorter. Fishhook cactus is so small one can easily miss it hidden amid the rocks.

BUCKHORN CHOLLA
(STAGHORN CHOLLA)

Cylindropuntia acanthocarpa
(Engelm. & J. Bigelow) F. M. Knuth
var. *coloradensis* (L. D. Benson) Pinkava
Cactus Family (Cactaceae)

Buckhorn cholla is an upright, highly branched cactus with a branching pattern reminiscent of the antlers of a male deer. This pattern gives it an overall scraggly, open shrub appearance. Stem segments are generally longer than 6 inches, which may help to distinguish this plant from Silver cholla, which has shorter and stouter stem segments. The light-brown spines cluster in groups of 12 to 21 but do not obscure the green plant surface. Lovely straw-yellow to dark-orange flowers appear in May to June. Buckhorn cholla grows in large stands in the Meadview area of LMNRA and along the road to Cottonwood Cove, but they are also scattered throughout the Creosotebush and Blackbrush communities.

TEDDYBEAR CHOLLA
(JUMPING CHOLLA)

Cylindropuntia bigelovii (Engelm.) F. M. Knuth
Cactus Family (Cactaceae)

Teddybear cholla is a fuzzy looking cactus but is neither fuzzy nor cuddly like a teddy bear and should be approached with caution. The readily detachable segments seem to jump out at you, which gives this plant its alternate common name, Jumping cholla. The barbed spines are painful to remove from skin and clothing, so pliers and a willing helper are often needed to extract them. Despite the spines, Cactus wrens nest in this plant and Desert woodrats use the spiny joints to protect their nests from predators. Teddybear cholla spreads by broken segments that fall on the ground and then grow new plants. Flowers are a light green and typically appear in May or June. Large stands of this cactus can be seen on the roads to Cottonwood Cove and to Nelsons Landing. Smaller, scattered stands are in the Newberry Mountains.

SILVER CHOLLA
(GOLDEN CHOLLA)

Cylindropuntia echinocarpa
(Engelm. & J. Bigelow) F. M. Knuth
Cactus Family (Cactaceae)

Silver cholla is an upright, branched, cylindrical cactus very similar in shape and distribution to Buckhorn cholla, except that Silver cholla's branches grow more densely packed together, and its stem segments are typically shorter and thicker. Each spine is enclosed in a silvery paper sheath, which gives the plant its common name, although sometimes the spines also appear golden in color. The flowers of Silver cholla are usually chartreuse green and appear from April to May. Silver cholla grows throughout LMNRA, particularly in the Creosotebush community.

DIAMOND CHOLLA
(PENCIL CHOLLA)

Cylindropuntia ramosissima
(Englem.) F. M. Knuth
Cactus Family (Cactaceae)

Diamond cholla is unusual because of its thin branches (a bit thicker than a pencil) that branch out from a thicker trunk. The spines are long and can make the plant appear to have a glow when the late afternoon sun backlights the stems. This plant can grow prostrate to the ground or more vertically. The branch segments can appear white, and the golden-tipped spines emerge singly, leaving much of the stem exposed. Yellow to orange flowers appear from May to June. The fleshy fruits are greenish.

COTTONTOP CACTUS (CLUSTERED BARREL CACTUS)

Echinocactus polycephalus Engelm.
& J. M. Bigelow var. *polycephalus*
Cactus Family (Cactaceae)

Cottontop cactus stems resemble Barrel cactus but grow in tight clusters, typically on south-facing hillsides. Each stem can resemble a basketball in size and shape. The flowers are yellow and can be hidden in spines at the top of the cactus. The name Cottontop comes from the cotton-like fibers produced by the fruits that develop from the flowers in a crown around the top of each stem. Look for this plant in rocky places in the Creosotebush community and the Meadview section of LMNRA.

HEDGEHOG CACTUS

Echinocereus engelmannii (Englem.) Lem.
Cactus Family (Cactaceae)

Hedgehog cactus is one of the most beautiful cacti of our region when it is in flower. Clusters of cylindrical stems form mounds that can all flower at once in the spring, creating a brilliant show of magenta petals clustered around a contrasting yellow mass of stamens and a green stigma. Another name for this plant is Strawberry hedgehog cactus, due to its red fruits, which are sweet and are eaten by birds and rodents. Spines on the stems can be multicolored, from yellow to pink, gray, or even black on the same plant. The species name, *engelmannii*, honors George Engelmann, a nineteenth-century botanist whose early work on North American cacti is still considered important today.

BARREL CACTUS
(CALIFORNIA BARREL CACTUS)

Ferocactus cylindraceus (Engelm.) Orcutt
Cactus Family (Cactaceae)

Barrel cactus is sought for landscaping, so it is monitored for poaching in LMNRA by the insertion of a chip that tracks illegally poached plants. The juicy, pulpy interior is sometimes consumed by desert wildlife but is too bitter for humans, who are unlikely to be able to quench their thirst from it. The flattened spines cluster in groups of 10 to 15. The central spine in each group is curved or hooked and thicker than the straighter, thinner, bristle-like spines on the outer edges of the spine cluster. Vertical ribs run the length of the stem. Yellow flowers form near the crown at the top of the plant from April to May and are followed by fleshy, yellow, spine-free fruits.

DEVIL CHOLLA
(PARISH'S CLUB-CHOLLA)

Grusonia parishii (Orcutt) Pinkava
Cactus Family (Cactaceae)

Devil cholla is easily overlooked because of its ground-hugging and spreading habit. However, the long, stiff spines can be crippling for anyone who accidentally steps on one. The stems are club-shaped and bear approximately 15 dense, thick spines per cluster, often obscuring the stems, which gives rise to its common name. The inner petals of the flowers are yellow and may have reddish stripes. Yellow, fleshy, spine-less fruits follow the May to June flowering. Flower photo by Pat Leary.

FISHHOOK CACTUS

Mammillaria tetrancistra Englem.
Cactus Family (Cactaceae)

Fishhook cactus is uncommonly seen in LMNRA, but a delight to encounter. This cactus only grows a few inches tall. The single to several stems have 40 to 60 spines per cluster, nearly covering the stem from view. The spine clusters grow at the tip of the projections (areole) of the stem, like the nipples of mammals, giving rise to the name of the genus. Most of the spines are white and radiate out from the cluster, while some of the central spines are longer and curved with dark, hooked tips that resemble a fishhook. The flowers (April to July) are pink to rose colored and seem to be too large to come from such a small cactus. Flowers are followed by bright red fruits, about 1-inch long, with a dry cleft at the top.

BEAVERTAIL

Opuntia basilaris Engelm. & J. M. Bigelow
Cactus Family (Cactaceae)

Beavertail is one of the easiest cacti to identify because of its flattened, blue-gray pads that look like the tails of beavers. Also, this cactus does not have stiff spines like others in the cactus family of plants, but instead has short, tiny spines called glochids. The glochids are barbed and can easily lodge in one's skin. Once in your skin, glochids are difficult to remove, so avoid touching these plants without protection. Beavertail is probably the most common cactus in LMNRA and occurs in most plant communities. Numerous pink or magenta flowers can cover the upper edges of the uppermost pads in April, typically after the spring wildflower display. A wet spring can result in an abundance of flowers on plants that, perhaps weeks before, looked dried and shriveled. Beavertails can serve as nurse plants, protecting grasses and wildflowers from being eaten by animals.

GRIZZLY BEAR PRICKLY PEAR (MOJAVE PRICKLY PEAR)

Opuntia polyacantha var. *erinacea*
(Engelm. & J. M. Bigelow) B. D. Parfitt
Cactus Family (Cactaceae)

Grizzly bear prickly pear cactus gets its name from the long, hair-like spines that somewhat resemble the fur on a brown grizzly bear. There can be as many as 24 brown to white spines per cluster. The spines may be rigid or flexible and thread-like. The density of these white, brown, or gray spines often obscure the pads. Flowers range from pure yellow to rose-tinged, peach-colored, or pink. Fruits are spiny and reddish green.

PYGMY BARREL CACTUS (JOHNSON'S BEE-HIVE CACTUS)

Sclerocactus johnsonii (Engelm.) N. P. Taylor
Cactus Family (Cactaceae)

This delightful, small cactus often goes unnoticed until the flowers appear. The reddish spines and small size help blend the cactus into the rocky terrain. The Pigmy barrel cactus is a cylindrical cactus that typically grows only inches tall. Its curved, thick spines cross over each other, covering and protecting the surface of the plant, but do not differ in shape and thickness, unlike the spines of Barrel cactus. The plant has numerous ribs, which are often wrinkled in appearance. Flowers appear in the spring and are either magenta or yellow.

Yuccas

The yuccas and, in particular, Joshua tree, are icons of the Mojave Desert with their dramatic shapes that help define the desert vistas. They also support many other species, including unique moth pollinators and rodents that eat their seeds.

BEARGRASS
(BIGELOW'S NOLINA)

Nolina bigelovii (Torr.) S. Watson
Agave Family (Agavaceae) or
Asparagus Family (Asparagaceae)

Beargrass loosely resembles a grass with its long, thin leaves. Beargrass has a rosette of large, leathery leaves, as with a yucca, but produces a tall flowering stalk that is covered with hundreds of small white flowers in late spring. The leaves of Beargrass have been used for basketry by some Native Americans. You can see this plant at the high point of Christmas Tree Pass.

BANANA YUCCA

Yucca baccata Torr. var. *baccata*
Agave Family (Agavaceae) or
Asparagus Family (Asparagaceae)

The common name comes from this plant's banana-shaped fruit that hang pendulously from the inflorescence stalk. Paiute Indians and others would eat the fruit fresh, roasted, or dried. The fibers and leaves were also used in construction and fabrics. In addition to reproducing by seed, Banana yucca reproduces vegetatively by way of basal bud sprouts and rhizomes. Vegetative reproduction enables it to survive fire. One can find this plant along Christmas Tree Pass and in the Meadview area of LMNRA, particularly in Blackbrush or Joshua tree communities. It is readily distinguished from our other yuccas because it sits close to the ground and does not have a trunk. The clusters of creamy-white, bell-shaped flowers appear on stalks from April to June.

JOSHUA TREE

Yucca brevifolia Engelm.
Agave Family (Agavaceae) or
Asparagus Family (Asparagaceae)

Joshua tree derives its name from early Mormon settlers who thought the upward arching branches reminded them of the Biblical story of Joshua with his arms raised up to the sky in prayer. Joshua trees can grow to over 15 feet tall in LMNRA. Historically, giant sloths likely helped disperse the seeds. Today, rodents have assumed that role. Joshua trees and our other native yuccas are pollinated by specific moth species that live in the flowers, actively pollinate the flowers by stuffing pollen onto the stigma of the flower, and then lay their eggs in the developing fruits. The developing seeds provide food for the moths' larvae. Joshua trees are visually dominant where they occur. In LMNRA, they are only found in the Meadview area. To see them, take the worthwhile, short walk through the Arizona Joshua Tree Forest at the junction of Pearce Ferry Road and Diamond Bar Road.

MOJAVE YUCCA

Yucca schidigera Ortgies
Agave Family (Agavaceae) or
Asparagus Family (Asparagaceae)

Mojave yucca is probably the most common yucca in LMNRA. You can find it in Creosotebush, Blackbrush, and Joshua tree communities. Mojave yuccas rarely branch but do tend to grow in clusters of stems from the same parent. The green, bayonet-like leaves have noticeable fibers along their margins that were used by Native Americans to make rope, sandals, and baskets. The flower stalks emerge from the top of the plant from April to May. The flowering stalks can extend 2 to 4 feet and are covered with conspicuous cream-colored flowers, followed by fibrous fruits.

Sedges and Grasses

Sedge and grass species number over 70 in LMNRA, so our illustrated sample of 14 common species is a fraction of what one can find and identify, with patience and a hand lens. We illustrate some of the tallest, like California sawgrass, and some of the shortest, like Fluffgrass. We also include both native species such as Big galleta and nonnative invasive species such as Red brome and Cheatgrass. These latter two species are partly responsible for the increase in wildfires in the Mojave Desert.

CALIFORNIA SAWGRASS (TWIG RUSH)

Cladium californicum (S. Watson) O'Neill
Sedge Family (Cyperaceae)

Despite its name, California sawgrass is not a grass but a sedge. Sedges superficially resemble grasses with their slender stalks and elongated leaves, but sedges generally have triangular and solid stems, whereas grasses have rounded, hollow stems. In keeping with its name, however, California sawgrass has sharp-toothed serrated margins on the leaves that contain silica and are capable of drawing blood from the bare arm or leg of anyone who tries to pass through a cluster of leaves. Look for this tall plant around Rogers Spring, where it is abundant.

AMERICAN BULRUSH (OLNEY'S THREE-SQUARE BULRUSH)

Schoenoplectus americanus (Pers.) Schinz & R. Keller
Sedge Family (Cyperaceae)

American bulrush is a sedge that can be spotted around Rogers, Blue Point, Sacaton, and Grapevine Springs. The plant is somewhat protected from fire because it grows near or in shallow water and has underground stems (rhizomes) that are usually about 6 inches below the soil surface. It can reproduce by seed (sexually) and propagate vegetatively by sprouts from the rhizome. American bulrush was widely used by Native Americans in basket and hat-making. The seeds are rich in protein and are eaten by both waterfowl and, formerly, humans. The density of stands of American bulrush provide cover and protection for many birds and small mammals.

PURPLE THREEAWN

Aristida purpurea Nutt.
Grass Family (Poaceae)

Purple threeawn grows on dry slopes and in well-drained shrublands and disturbed areas such as roadsides. The common and botanical names of this plant cover its diagnostic description very well: *Aristida* refers to the Latin for awn, and *purpurea* to the purplish coloration of the inflorescence. Purple threeawn references the three separate awns extending like legs of a three-legged stool out of the top of the tiny seed. This grass has spread widely in LMNRA over the last twenty years and lines Northshore Road in places.

RED BROME

Bromus rubens L.
Grass Family (Poaceae)

Red brome is a nonnative invasive species that is widespread throughout the Mojave Desert. The annual grass is green in spring months but with the onset of warm weather it persists in the landscape as dry stems, which can promote the spread of fire. The long awns of mature Red brome fruits and seeds are harmful to native animals and livestock. The awned seeds readily penetrate fur, socks, and pants and can be dispersed by animals and people walking through the area. You will encounter this grass almost anywhere you go in LMNRA.

CHEATGRASS

Bromus tectorum L.
Grass Family (Poaceae)

Cheatgrass is a nonnative invasive grass that has become much more common in LMNRA over the last twenty years. Because Cheatgrass germinates after early autumn rains, it can establish a root system and commence growth in late winter months, giving it a competitive advantage over native wildflowers. Cheatgrass is then able to draw down soil moisture and nutrients early in the season before native species break dormancy. Once established, Cheatgrass increases the size of its population at the expense of native species by accelerating fire cycles, as does its relative, Red brome. Cheatgrass primarily grows in open, disturbed areas but is becoming more common in undisturbed desert as well.

FLUFFGRASS

Dasyochloa pulchella (Kunth) Rydb.
Grass Family (Poaceae)

Fluffgrass is a low, densely tufted perennial grass with many wiry stems and grows to no more than several inches tall. In places, it can look as though the ground is covered with little, white, spikey balls of fluff. Fluffgrass is found on dry rocky slopes, gravelly soils, and desert flats. *Pulchella* from Latin means "beautiful and small." Look for it at Northshore Summit Trail.

SALTGRASS

Distichlis spicata (L.) Greene
Grass Family (Poaceae)

Saltgrass grows in the Alkali shrub community around springs such as Rogers and Blue Point. This grass is able to excrete salt from its tissues through salt glands, which then make the soil more saline. However, when growing in hyper-saline areas, it can grow in a dwarfed form. The encrusted salt on the leaves may reflect light off the leaves, thereby reducing heat load and water loss. Native Americans collected salt deposited on the leaves to use on food and for medicinal purposes. The leaves were dried on a mat and then beaten with sticks and winnowed in a basket. The leaves were also used in basketry, matting, rope, sandals, and for other utilitarian purposes. Recently, Saltgrass has been used for erosion and dust control.

SIXWEEKS FESCUE (SIXWEEKS GRASS)

Festuca octoflora Walter
Grass Family (Poaceae)

Sixweeks fescue is a shallow rooted, tufted, annual grass with upright stems that can grow up to 1 foot tall, but is usually much shorter. This grass grows in early spring in sandy and rocky soils in the Creosotebush community. The common name may refer to the 6 weeks of palatability the plant provides cattle before it dries, although the plant is usually so small here at LMNRA that it is unlikely to have much forage value. This native grass is common throughout the United States.

BIG GALLETA

Hilaria rigida (Thurb.) Benth. ex Scribn.
Grass Family (Poaceae)

Big galleta is a large, perennial bunchgrass common on sandy areas and dunes of LMNRA. It can stabilize loose and shifting soils on sand dunes, which makes it a good candidate for revegetation efforts. The stems of Big galleta are unusual for a grass because they are solid between the nodes, whereas most grasses have hollow stems. The flowers (May to June) are produced in serial clusters of spikelets (grass flowers). After the seeds disperse and the spikelets fall away, the wavy, zigzag inflorescence stalks that remain are a diagnostic feature of this grass.

COMMON REED

Phragmites australis (Cav.) Steud.
Grass Family (Poaceae)

Common reed forms tall stands along rivers in LMNRA and is especially dense along Las Vegas Wash. Common reed was a very useful plant in the economic life of Native Americans in Southern Nevada and the Mojave Desert. The stalks were used for making arrows and pipes, and archaeological arrow and dart shafts of the stalks have been found in Gypsum and Newberry Caves. The stalks were also a major source of sugar, derived from the sweet exudate of plant-sucking insects. The dried secretions were gathered up, rolled into balls, and then eaten as candy.

MEDITERRANEAN GRASS
Schismus barbatus (L.) Thell.
Grass Family (Poaceae)

Mediterranean grass is a nonnative invasive grass from Eurasia that has spread throughout the southwestern US and is now naturalized in the dry, open disturbed places of LMNRA and the Mojave Desert. Like Red brome, Mediterranean grass germinates quickly after winter rains and can outcompete native wildflowers for water. This grass also contributes to the replacement of desert shrublands to grasslands after fires. It can be found nearly everywhere in LMNRA.

ALKALI SACATON
Sporobolus airoides (Torr.) Torr.
Grass Family (Poaceae)

Alkali sacaton is found near springs in LMNRA such as Grapevine Spring. This large, perennial bunchgrass can tolerate both drought and periodic flooding. It has been used for planting in the campground at Willow Beach. Leaf blades have a prominent mid-vein and are stiff and tapered to a long point.

RICEGRASS
(SAND RICE GRASS)

Stipa hymenoides Roem. & Schult.
Grass Family (Poaceae)

Ricegrass is a perennial bunchgrass most often found on sandy soils. It was an important early summer food utilized by Native Americans of the region. Bunches of grass would be gathered in piles, beaten with sticks to loosen the seeds, and winnowed in basket trays. Seeds were often roasted and pounded into flour and stored for later use. Stands of Ricegrass were occasionally managed by sowing seeds and burning areas to stimulate growth. Ricegrass is the State Grass of Nevada. Look for it on sand dunes and at Redstone.

SOUTHERN CATTAIL

Typha domingensis Pers.
Cattail Family (Typhaceae)

Cattails are obligate wetland plants tolerant of perennial flooding and moderate salinity. Look for Southern cattail at Rogers Spring, along Las Vegas Wash, and in calm shoreline areas like Cottonwood Cove and Nevada Telephone Cove. When the inflorescence is ripe, the heads disintegrate into a slowly billowing, cottony fluff. Southern cattail is an important food source for small mammals and waterfowl. It was extensively used by Native Americans. The stalks and leaves were used to thatch homes, and the fluff used for insulation. The leaves were used for bedding and matting, the rhizomes eaten raw or cooked (like potatoes), and the seeds made into flat cakes.

Aquatic Plants

We include two aquatic plants that are particularly abundant along the shorelines of Lakes Mead and Mohave. As we describe, one is prickly and one is not. You will quickly find out which is which if you boat, swim, or wade in shallow areas, particularly in late summer and autumn.

SPINY NAIAD
(HOLLY-LEAVED WATER-NYMPH)

Najas marina L.
Waterweed Family (Hydrocharitaceae)

Boaters and swimmers in Lake Mead may be familiar with this submerged plant that grows on the bottom of the lake in shallow areas during summer. The leaves have spiny edges that will prick your skin. A naiad in Greek mythology was a female water nymph, or spirit, that lived in fresh water. Where this plant gathers on the shoreline and starts to decompose, it can have the fragrance of seaweed.

FENNEL-LEAF PONDWEED
(SAGO PONDWEED)

Stukenia pectinata (L.) Börner
Pondweed Family (Potamogetonaceae)

Here is another aquatic plant that you are likely to find on your boat prop or while swimming in Lake Mead. Fennel-leaf pondweed is not prickly on your skin and can be seen waving gently in shallow water in summer. It is perennial but can be seen as a fine grass along the bottom of shallow areas of the lake or in masses in late summer. Fennel-leaf pondweed has upright flowering stems with whorls of flowers and fruits that just touch the surface of the water. Pondweeds are an important food source for water birds.

Wildflowers

Wildflowers are best seen in LMNRA from February to May following a wet winter. On such occasions, they can provide magnificent color to the desert landscape. Some wildflowers also bloom from August to November following substantial monsoonal rains in late summer. During more typically dry weather, one sometimes must search for wet spots, such as around springs or lakeshores, to find something in flower. We organize the wildflowers by color (white and cream; yellow and orange; red, pink, and magenta; blue and purple; and inconspicuous). However, the colors intergrade and can even change as a flower ages. The majority of the wildflowers are white or yellow; orange and blue are rather uncommon flower colors. Check the cross-reference guide at the end of wildflowers for a list of plants of different life forms that have similar flower colors.

WOOLLY BLUESTAR
(SMALL-LEAVED AMSONIA)

Amsonia tomentosa Torr. & Frém.
Dogbane Family (Apocynaceae)

Woolly bluestar is known for two distinct forms: leaves that are green, smooth, and hairless (glabrous) or are grey and woolly (covered in short, white hairs). Like many plants in the Dogbane family, Woolly bluestar stems exude a milky sap when broken. Native Americans extracted the fibers from the stems of the plant to braid them into twine, straps, and blankets. It is a much-branched herbaceous perennial that grows from a woody base. This wildflower has white to light-blue tubular flowers (March to May) that have petals that spread in five lobes. The fruits are narrow and constricted, each segment generally containing a single seed. Look for this wildflower along Christmas Tree Pass.

GRAVEL GHOST

Atrichoseris platyphylla (A. Gray) A. Gray
Sunflower Family (Asteraceae)

Gravel ghost is included in a tribe of sunflower plants that have milky sap and white ray flowers. The plants are hairless, with fleshy basal leaves that are mottled green and purple. The spindly stems topped by the showy flowers (March to May) resemble an expanded parachute or ghosts floating in the air. Look for this plant on rocky hillsides along Northshore Road.

PEBBLE PINCUSHION

Chaenactis carphoclinia A. Gray
Sunflower Family (Asteraceae)

Pebble pincushion is found mostly on gravelly and desert pavement areas of the Cresosotebush community. It is usually not abundant in any one place but can be scattered across the landscape. It has green-purplish phyllaries that are long-pointed at the top and turn reddish at the time of flowering. The heads of the tightly packed disk flowers are often pink.

FREMONT PINCUSHION

Chaenactis fremontii A. Gray
Sunflower Family (Asteraceae)

Fremont pincushion is abundant in spring in many areas of LMNRA in Creosotebush communities. It frequently occurs in washes and under and around shrubs, often with Desert dandelion. The flower heads have only disk flowers, but the outer layer of flowers are asymmetrical. Achenes (fruits) have a stiff pappus of four papery scales. The flower bracts (phyllaries) are usually green and have a pointed tip. This wildflower can spread rapidly from seed and can be grown in rock gardens. Look for it in abundance at Redstone.

DESERT PINCUSHION

Chaenactis stevioides Hook. & Arn.
Sunflower Family (Asteraceae)

Look for Desert pincushion on sandy soils. The leaves are divided, greyish, and covered with fine hairs. The flower heads have only disk flowers. The outer ring of flowers are asymmetrical. You can tell this plant from the Fremont pincushion because the phyllaries are covered with short, fine hairs and blunt at the tip. Pincushions are a valuable food source for the southwestern Desert tortoise.

WHITE WOOLLY DAISY (WOOLLY SUNFLOWER)

Eriophyllum lanosum (A. Gray) A. Gray
Sunflower Family (Asteraceae)

The common (woolly) and scientific (*lanosum*) names for this plant both refer to the dense white hairs that resemble wool. White woolly daisy stems are very short, just an inch or two from the ground level, and produce a single flower head of white ray flowers and yellow disk flowers per stem (February to May). It is widespread throughout LMNRA. In some areas it can become so abundant that it looks like the ground is covered in snow.

DESERT STAR

Monoptilon bellioides (A. Gray) H. M. Hall
Sunflower Family (Asteraceae)

Desert star is a good example of a "belly plant" because it seems to barely emerge from the sandy or stony soil surface where it grows in LMNRA. This annual has radiating stems that give an overall circular appearance. Desert star leaves have stiff hairs and grow beneath a large head of flowers (January to May) that close at night. A second species of *Monoptilon* in LMNRA (*M. bellidiforme*) is distinguished by the shape of the fruits (achenes), otherwise the two species are nearly identical.

ROCK DAISY
(EMORY'S ROCK DAISY)

Perityle emoryi Torr.
Sunflower Family (Asteraceae)

Rock daisy commonly grows in crevices on cliff faces and near boulders in washes and canyons. These habitats allow the plant's roots to tap into pooled water. Overhanging rocks also provide protection from the searing summer sun. The plant was named after Major W. H. Emory, from the US Army Corps of Topographic Engineers. He helped survey the new border with Mexico after the Gadsen Purchase of 1854, which provided land for the Southern Pacific Railroad. The leaves are distinctly palm-shaped and the flowers appear in spring and autumn, depending on moisture availability. Look for this wildflower in rocky, shaded canyons, such as Owl Canyon.

ODORA
(SLENDER PORELEAF)

Porophyllum gracile Benth.
Sunflower Family (Asteraceae)

Odora, a bluish-green subshrub, has a pungent odor that comes from numerous purple glands on the bracts, leaves, and stems. These glands emit several volatile compounds that likely repel potential insect herbivores. The flower heads (March to October) are narrow and are composed of 20 to 30 white disc flowers with red anthers. A pink or purplish curling style protrudes above the petals, giving the flower head the appearance of being a single pink flower. Look for this plant in sandy areas, such as Redstone.

DESERT CHICORY

Rafinesquia neomexicana A. Gray
Sunflower Family (Asteraceae)

Desert chicory is a hairless, weak-stemmed annual with milky sap that grows up to but usually less than 2 feet tall, often within the canopy of other shrubs that support it and protect it from herbivory and water loss. It can fool you; you think you have found a lovely flowering shrub, and on closer inspection find that you have found Desert chicory growing up and flowering inside a shrub. The bases of the deeply lobed leaves clasp the stem. The underside of its ray flowers (February to June) is sometimes streaked with purple. Constantine Samuel Rafinesque (1783–1840) was an eccentric genius who made significant contributions to the fields of botany, zoology, geology, anthropology, and linguistics.

NARROWLEAF CRYPTANTHA
Cryptantha angustifolia (Torr.) Greene
Borage Family (Boraginaceae)

There are eighteen species of *Cryptantha* in LMNRA and they can be hard to distinguish. Members of this genus are collectively referred to as popcorn flowers, forget-me-nots, or cat's-eyes. They tend to have many narrow stems and bristly leaves. The white flowers are individually very small; *kryptos* refers to something hidden, and *anthos* refers to flowers. The flowers grow on one side of a curved cyme inflorescence that elongates with age. The fruits (nutlets) in this genus are small and are best examined with a hand lens. Narrowleaf cryptantha is one of the more common and early flowering plants in the spring.

NEVADA CRYPTANTHA
Cryptantha nevadensis A. Nelson
& P. B. Kenn. var. *nevadensis*
Borage Family (Boraginaceae)

Nevada cryptantha can be distinguished by its cloud of bristles along its stem and leaves and its elongated bristly fruits. This annual plant has a straggly, ground-hugging habit. Nevada cryptantha has fruits composed of four narrow nutlets with pointed tips and warty surfaces. Look for this wildflower in sheltered rocky and gravelly places.

WINGED-NUT CRYPTANTHA
Cryptantha pterocarya (Torr.) Greene
Borage Family (Boraginaceae)

No magnification is needed to identify Winged-nut cryptantha. It is characterized by its upright habit and its four recognizably swollen, yellow-green fruits that form beneath its tiny, white flowers. As its name suggests (*pteron* refers to winged), the nutlets have sharp, wing-like extensions. Winged-nut cryptantha can grow over 1 foot tall and, like other Cryptanthas, has bristly hairs along its stem and leaves.

SCENTED CRYPTANTHA
(UTAH CRYPTANTHA)
Cryptantha utahensis (A. Gray) Greene
Borage Family (Boraginaceae)

Scented cryptantha has an upright habit, and large, fragrant flowers clustered closely together. Where it blooms in abundance you can smell the flowers. It is one of the least bristly species of cryptantha found in LMNRA. The fruit is composed of one, or occasionally two, nutlets with sharp, knife-like margins.

FLATTENED COMBSEED
(WIDE-TOOTHED PECTOCARYA)

Pectocarya platycarpa (Munz &
I. M. Johnst.) Munz & I. M. Johnst.
Borage Family (Boraginaceae)

We show two of the four species of combseed in LMNRA. The combseeds are found straggling along the ground in LMNRA in the Creosotebush community. They are an important part of the small spring wildflowers and can be found in sandy washes, on rocky desert flats, and along roadsides. They all have tiny white flowers (February to May) but four noticeable fruits (nutlets) that enlarge and spread backward in the shape of a cross or butterfly. The margins of the nutlets are differentially toothed and provide a diagnostic character to distinguish species. Flattened combseed has very broad pale and toothed margins around each nutlet.

BENT COMBSEED
(ARCHED-NUT PECTOCARYA)

Pectocarya recurvata I. M. Johnst.
Borage Family (Boraginaceae)

Bent combseed has small white inconspicuous flowers and fruit (nutlets) in a cross or butterfly shape. It can be distinguished from its relative, Flattened combseed, by its finely toothed fruit margins that are strongly arched backward (recurved). The name, *Pectocarya,* comes from the Greek *pectos,* meaning "comb," and *karuan,* "nut."

CALIFORNIA MAN-ROOT

Marah fabacea (Naudin) Greene
Gourd Family (Cucurbitaceae)

California man-root's name refers to the resemblance of the root to a human figure, while *Marah* is Hebrew for "bitter." It is a perennial vine with five to seven lobed, heart-shaped leaves and a U-shape where the veins converge at the base of the leaf blade. The stems are hairy and have twining, threadlike structures (tendrils) that coil around stems of other plants for support. The spherical fruit, covered in prickles, can induce vomiting when ingested and has saponins that can be processed into a soapy extract. The plant grows along riverbanks, in shady canyons, and on seasonally moist soils. Look for this plant in Christmas Tree Pass and Gold Strike Canyon.

WHITE-MARGINED SPURGE (RATTLESNAKE WEED)

Chamaesyce albomarginata
(Torr. & A. Gray) Small
Spurge Family (Euphorbiaceae)

White-margined spurge is a common perennial herb and forms a ground-hugging mat of densely packed, forked stems that lack hairs and exude a milky sap when broken. The many small round leaves are opposite one another on the stem. The small flowers are highly modified structures composed of fused bracts forming a cup with a ring of burgundy-colored nectar glands and white petal-like bracts. Within each cup are 15 to 30 inconspicuous male flowers surrounding a single, stalked female flower. After fertilization, the female flower bears a three-angled capsule fruit. The entire structure mimics a single flower. White-margined spurge grows in open, gravelly areas and along roadsides.

SMALLSEED SANDMAT

Chamaesyce polycarpa (Benth.) Millsp.
Spurge Family (Euphorbiaceae)

Smallseed sandmat is a common perennial herb that can be either prostrate or erect with small, oval to round, opposite leaves. The flower heads are also small and have one female and 15 to 30 male flowers (February-November) surrounded by white to red bracts. The petal-like bracts can be large or almost nonexistent. Maroon to black glands are found at the base of the bracts. This wildflower is very common along roadsides and in disturbed habitats.

HELIOTROPE

Heliotropium curassavicum L. var.
oculatum (A. Heller) Tidestr.
Heliotrope Family (Heliotropiaceae)
or Borage Family (Boraginaceae)

Heliotropium comes from the Latin *helios* (sun) and *trope* (to turn), referring to the belief that the flowers turned to continuously face the arcing sun. Heliotrope is a bluish-green, fleshy perennial herb that often grows prostrate along the ground. The succulent, hairless leaves are wedge-shaped and the white-to-blue flowers (February to October) have yellow throats and grow in a dense cluster along a cyme inflorescence. Heliotrope grows in dry or moist saline or alkaline soils generally near springs, rivers, and shorelines in LMNRA. Look for it also in the drawdown zone around Boulder Basin.

ROCK NETTLE

Eucnide urens (A. Gray) Parry
Stickleaf Family (Loasaceae)

Rock nettle is a lovely perennial herb with a woody base and satiny, cream-colored flowers. It often grows at eye level in cracks on near-vertical rock surfaces, especially in shady canyons. It can become a large shrub on sand dunes. Hairs on its leaves secrete an irritant that causes a stinging rash and the barbed hairs can cause the leaves to cling to one's clothes. This is definitely a plant to avoid touching.

BLAZING STAR
(SPINY-HAIR BLAZING STAR)

Mentzelia tricuspis A. Gray
Stickleaf Family (Loasaceae)

Blazing star is an annual plant with stems that grow densely packed, and has long leaves that have toothed margins and barbed hairs. The five-parted flowers (March to May) are creamy white to pale yellow. The stamens appear two-lobed at the tips. Despite its close resemblance to Rock nettle, Blazing star will not sting you. Blazing star grows in sand or gravel, particularly in washes and canyon edges in the Creosotebush community.

BROWNEYED PRIMROSE

Chylismia claviformis (Torr. & Frém.) Heller
Evening-Primrose Family (Onagraceae)

Browneyed primrose is one of the most abundant and widespread spring wildflowers. The cluster of white flowers (March to May) grow on sometimes nodding stalks, and the flowers have a cup to which the petals and stamens are attached. The center of the cup can be red or brown, which gives the wildflower its common name. Look for this wildflower in sandy washes or under shrubs in good wildflower years. Photo by Kathlyn Powell.

DUNE PRIMROSE (BIRDCAGE OENOTHERA)

Oenothera deltoides Torr. & Frém.
Evening-Primrose Family (Onagraceae)

Dune primrose is a sprawling annual that, because of its large leaves and flowers, looks incongruous in a desert, let alone on dry, sandy soils. Yet it taps enough moisture from water sources beneath the sand (particularly on the lee side of dunes) to support its large leaves and flowers. The leaves are usually lobed and the flowers (April to May) emerge from nodding buds. Flowers open in the evening and wilt during the day and can turn pink. The flowers are large enough to look like discarded tissues along sandy roadsides. The outer stems of this plant often curl upward and inward when they dry, forming a distinctive, basket or bird cage. Look for this wildflower in sandy places.

WHITE DESERT GOLD

Leptosiphon chrysanthus J. M. Porter & R. Patt.
subsp. *decorus* (A. Gray) J. M. Porter & R. Patt.
Phlox Family (Polemoniaceae)

White desert gold is a small, annual herb with a thread-like, reddish stem that grows 2 to 3 inches tall and has five small, linear leaves. Its funnel-shaped flowers have flaring petals (March to June) with an obvious, black center. This plant covers the ground along the trail to Grapevine Canyon in good wildflower years.

HUMBLE GILIA

Linanthus demissus (A. Gray) Greene
Phlox Family (Polemoniaceae)

Humble gilia is an annual belly plant with creeping stems, tiny, linear leaves, and bell-shaped white to yellow-green, fragrant flowers (March to May). The flowers have several parallel, purple-to-red streaks on the inner base of the petals. Look for this wildflower on desert pavement, rocky places, and in sandy washes in the Creosotebush community.

SKELETON BUCKWHEAT
(FLAT-TOPPED SKELETON WEED)

Eriogonum deflexum Torr. var. *deflexum*
Buckwheat Family (Polygonaceae)

Skeleton buckwheat is a common annual with many branched, hairless stems that end in a flat top about 1 foot off the ground. The basal leaves are hairy and heart-shaped and the flowers (April to October) are small and typically hang down from the branches. Skeleton buckwheat stems turn reddish brown with age, and from a distance one can see whole hillsides and road banks tinged red brown, particularly along Northshore Road. There are 15 species of *Eriogonum* in LMNRA and over one hundred in the southwestern US. We have included Desert buckwheat in the shrub section and Desert trumpet and Little desert trumpet in the yellow and orange flower section. Skeleton buckwheat is common on disturbed sites throughout LMNRA.

YERBA MANSA
(LIZARD TAIL)

Anemopsis californica (Nutt.) Hook. & Arn.
Lizard Tail Family (Saururaceae)

Yerba mansa is a striking plant that is common in moist alkaline or saline soil around seeps, springs, and marshes. It is a perennial herb that grows from stout, woody rhizomes and creeping runners. The aromatic leaves come in two sizes: long, basal leaves and shorter stem leaves. The stalked inflorescence consists of a ring of large white bracts that appears to be a single flower of white (sometimes reddish) petals. The true flowers (March to September) above the bracts are clustered in a persistent conical spike of about 100 flowers per spike. When dry, the stalk and inflorescence age to a rusty, reddish-brown color. Yerba mansa has been used for a variety of medicinal purposes by Native Americans. Look for this wildflower at Rogers and Blue Point Springs.

SACRED DATURA
(JIMSON WEED)

Datura wrightii Regel
Nightshade Family (Solanaceae)

Sacred datura is sometimes cultivated for its large (up to 8 inches long), trumpet-shaped flowers (April to October). The flowers have a sweet fragrance, open at night, and are pollinated by sphinx moths. The fruits are 1 to 2 inches in diameter and covered with spines with flat, tan seeds inside. The large leaves are typically cool to the touch, even during hot summer days, due to evaporative cooling from water loss on the leaf surface. The plant can grow several feet tall and cover up to 50 square feet of ground. Although once used by Native Americans as a hallucinogen in religious ceremonies, all plant parts are toxic to ingest and potentially fatal.

DESERT TOBACCO

Nicotiana obtusifolia M. Martens & Galeotti
Nightshade Family (Solanaceae)

Desert tobacco is a common perennial herb that grows as a robust clump of tall stems covered with sticky glands. The leaves clasp the stem at the base. Tubular flowers (March to June) grow in clusters at the ends of branches. Desert tobacco can often be found in gravelly washes and canyons in LMNRA. As with Sacred datura, this plant was once used ceremonially by Native Americans; however, all parts are toxic.

DESERT MARIGOLD

Baileya multiradiata Torr.
Sunflower Family (Asteraceae)

Desert marigold is an abundant, colorful wildflower found throughout LMNRA, particularly along roadsides. It is often gray-woolly in appearance due to an abundance of hairs on its stems and leaves. Its yellow flowers grow on long naked stalks well above the leaves. Its abundant seeds are an important food source for rodents. When sown in seed mixes with other native species for restoration of abandoned roads, this plant can dominate, reducing the diversity of other plant species. The golden-yellow flowers appear under favorably moist conditions from March to October. The species name, *multiradiata,* refers to its many spreading ray flowers.

SUNRAY

Enceliopsis argophylla (D. C. Eaton) A. Nelson
Sunflower Family (Asteraceae)

Sunray, with its delightfully large and showy flowers and silvery leaves, provides a sharp contrast of lush growth against the austere and nearly barren background of the white gypsum mounds. The leaves use evaporative cooling to survive the hot desert temperatures. This plant is often found in association with other gypsum-tolerant plants such as Las Vegas bearpoppy, Palmer's phacelia, and Thurber's sandpaper plant. Look for this plant along Lakeshore and Northshore Roads.

WOOLLY DAISY
(WALLACE'S WOOLLY DAISY)

Eriophyllum wallacei (A. Gray) A. Gray
Sunflower Family (Asteraceae)

Woolly daisy plants often form colorful yellow carpets on sandy and fine gravelly surfaces. They are a good example of a belly plant because they are best viewed from a prone position. The plants have a dense cover of white, felt-like hairs that help reflect heat from the sun. During dry years, plants may only produce a single flower head and a few tiny leaves, but in wetter years, they branch and produce many flower heads of yellow ray and disk flowers. Look for this plant in abundance in gravelly washes throughout LMNRA in the spring months.

DESERT SUNFLOWER
(DESERT GOLD)

Geraea canescens Torr. & A. Gray
Sunflower Family (Asteraceae)

Desert sunflower is one of the most widespread and consistent plants to bloom in LMNRA and is particularly obvious along roadsides. Phyllaries of the flower heads are green with white, fringed edges, which makes them look striped from a distance. Flowers generally appear on rocky hillsides from February to May and occasionally again in wet autumns. It provides an important food source for both pollinators (bees and moths) and seed eaters (birds and rodents).

DESERT DANDELION

Malacothrix glabrata (D. C. Eaton) A. Gray
Sunflower Family (Asteraceae)

Desert dandelion is a common annual that can form dense carpets of flowers during wet springs and provides an important food source for the Desert tortoise. Flower heads are light lemon yellow and made up of all ray flowers. Look for the red tips of inner ray flowers in the center of some flower heads. Look for it on open flats, in sandy washes, and around shrubs during wet spring seasons. It also grows in disturbed areas such as abandoned roads and vacant lots.

CHINCHWEED (FETID MARIGOLD)

Pectis papposa Harv. & A. Gray var. *papposa*
Sunflower Family (Asteraceae)

The delight of seeing Chinchweed is that it arrives in yellow brilliance (August to November) at a time when most other annuals in the Mojave Desert have dried up and gone to seed, leaving a less colorful landscape. It relies on monsoonal, late-summer rains for germination and survival. Chinchweed is also easily identified because of its reddish stems that spread horizontally along the ground and its spicy aroma. In wet autumns, it can turn the desert landscape into a golden carpet.

GROUNDSEL (THREADLEAF RAGWORT)

Senecio flaccidus Less.
Sunflower Family (Asteraceae)

Groundsel grows throughout LMNRA, particularly in washes. This wildflower is a subshrub because it grows from a woody taproot. Plants can grow to a height of up to 3 feet tall. Flower heads have bright yellow ray and disk flowers. Ray flower petals are narrow, which makes the flower head look like a child's drawing of a sun. Flowers can appear both in the spring and in the autumn after late summer rains. The many soft hairs (pappus) at the top of the fruits (achenes) are the likely origin of *Senecio* from the Latin *senex* (old man).

NEVADA GOLDENROD (SHOWY GOLDENROD)

Solidago spectabilis (D. C. Eaton) A. Gray
Sunflower Family (Asteraceae)

This lovely perennial grows up to 6 feet tall and is found along riverbanks and moist, alkaline areas, such as at Rogers and Blue Point Springs. The lowest leaves on the stem are the largest, and they are progressively smaller in size toward the top of the stem. The flower heads (July to September) are made up of obvious disk flowers and ray flowers with tiny petals.

DOGWEED

Thymophylla pentachaeta (DC.) Small
var. *belenidium* (DC.) Strother
Sunflower Family (Asteraceae)

Dogweed is a small, sometimes woody, aromatic plant (smelling like thyme, hence *Thymophylla*) that has conspicuous, amber-colored glands below its flowers and along the phyllaries. It grows mainly in a variety of dry habitats, including along roadsides, on rocky ridges, and in limestone soils. Look for this plant along Northshore Road.

FIDDLENECK
(DESERT FIDDLENECK)

Amsinckia tessellata A. Gray var. *tessellata*
Borage Family (Boraginaceae)

Fiddleneck is a common and early spring annual wildflower in LMNRA, particularly noticeable by its curled, nodding stem tips and one-sided cyme inflorescence. The plant bristles with dense, stiff hairs that can cause a rash when the plant is handled, so we recommend just admiring and not touching this wildflower. Fiddleneck grows throughout LMNRA, sometimes in large, extensive populations and can be found throughout the western US.

SAHARA MUSTARD
Brassica tournefortii Gouan
Mustard Family (Brassicaceae)

Sahara mustard is a nonnative plant (from the Mediterranean region) that invaded LMNRA in approximately 2003 to 2005, apparently from southern California. It crossed the Mojave Desert along roadways, suggesting that disturbed corridors were an important factor in its rapid spread. Active removal efforts by the National Park Service and perhaps genetic inbreeding led to smaller populations and fewer range expansions within about five years following its invasion into LMNRA. The leaves and stems have the smell of cabbage or radish and have stinging hairs. The small light yellow flowers have four petals and six stamens: the typical floral arrangement for all plants in the Mustard family. This plant's seed production is prolific, a typical characteristic of invasive plants. Look for it in disturbed areas, in the drawdown zone of Lake Mead, and along trails and roadsides in early spring.

FLIXWEED
(TANSY MUSTARD)
Descurainia sophia (L.) Prantl.
Mustard Family (Brassicaceae)

Flixweed is a nonnative annual from Eurasia that flowers throughout the summer and can grow 3 to 4 feet tall. It has narrow, hairy, gray-green, and deeply lobed leaves. It grows in a variety of habitats throughout LMNRA but is most likely seen in open, disturbed habitats. In wetter places, such as washes, it can form dense colonies.

BEADPOD

Physaria tenella (A. Nelson)
O'Kane & Al-Shehbaz
Mustard Family (Brassicaceae)

Beadpod has tiny, distinctive, bead-like fruits and the whole plant, like many mustards, has a tangy smell. Beadpod grows best on sandy soils but is also found in dry washes and growing up through other shrubs in early spring before most other wildflowers start flowering.

PRINCE'S PLUME

Stanleya pinnata (Pursh) Britton var. *pinnata*
Mustard Family (Brassicaceae)

Prince's plume is a showy, 2 to 5 foot tall perennial herb that grows in washes and canyons but also on dunes and rocky hillsides. The inflorescence has bright yellow flowers that mature first from the bottom and progress upward. The lower leaves are deeply lobed, while the upper leaves are not lobed. The dry, elongated fruits may remain on the flower stalk for many months after maturity. Prince's plume can accumulate selenium from the soil, making it toxic to livestock and humans.

COYOTE MELON

Cucurbita palmata S. Watson
Gourd Family (Cucurbitaceae)

Finding Coyote melon in LMNRA is always an occasion to wonder if one has accidentally stepped into somebody's garden. The large, deep-green lobed leaves, the big bell-shaped flowers, and the round, melon-like yellow fruits (gourds) do not look like most desert plants. When there is a ready source of moisture, such as in washes or drainage ditches, Coyote melon plants can get very large, making them even more obvious. Coyotes readily consume the fruits, and Native Americans used the gourds as ceremonial rattles.

DESERT BIRDFOOT TREFOIL (DEERVETCH)

Acmispon strigosus (Nutt.) Brouillet
Pea Family (Fabaceae)

Desert birdfoot trefoil is a fleshy annual with low growing and spreading stems. The leaves and stems are covered with dense hairs. The yellow, pea-shaped flowers appear in the spring. The mature fruits are purplish peapods about 1-inch long. It is most common in washes, sandy soils, and disturbed habitats such as roadsides.

WHITE-STEMMED BLAZING STAR (WHITE-STEMMED STICK-LEAF)

Mentzelia albicaulis (Hook.) Torr. & A. Gray
Stick-Leaf Family (Loasaceae)

The flowers of White-stemmed blazing star are perhaps less conspicuous than the distinctly white stems. The small yellow flowers and white stems set this wildflower apart from other plants in this family. All LMNRA wildflowers in this family have barbed hairs that will stick to clothing. It is tempting to want to make a boutonniere out of a flower, but please do not pick wildflowers in LMNRA.

SUNCUPS (GOLDEN EVENING-PRIMROSE)

Chylismia brevipes (A. Gray) Small
Evening-primrose Family (Onagraceae)

Suncups is both common and conspicuous among annual wildflowers and is one of the earliest to appear in the spring. It grows abundantly in washes and on gravelly hillsides. The morning opening of flowers differs from the sunset opening of the flowers of other plants in the Evening- primrose family. There are three species of *Chylismia* recorded in LMNRA, with some hybridization among them. Note the four petals and ball-like stigma on this wildflower. Large displays of this wildflower in wet spring seasons can be seen on the road to Willow Beach.

LAS VEGAS BEARPOPPY (BEARPAW POPPY)

Arctomecon californica Torr. & Frém.
Poppy Family (Papaveraceae)

Las Vegas bearpoppy is both lovely and rare, so it is a special treat to come across this plant. The flowers are delicate and pale yellow in color, and sit on stalks above the leaves (April–May). The basal rosette of silvery gray leaves are densely covered with hairs, which makes them look like a bear's paw. This wildflower is found only on gypsum soils, typically on old spring mounds such as are found near Blue Point Spring and several other locations along Northshore Road. The Las Vegas bearpoppy has been listed as critically endangered by the state of Nevada. Much of its habitat has been lost to urbanization, energy development, and mining. It is a short-lived perennial that can be abundant in some years and appear to completely vanish in others. Seeds need a long, cold, wet winter to trigger germination.

DESERT GOLD POPPY

Eschscholtzia glyptosperma Greene
Poppy Family (Papaveraceae)

Desert gold poppy is a common annual wildflower in LMNRA. Great masses of flowers can be seen on gravelly hillsides, washes, and slopes around springs throughout the Creosotebush community. It has basal leaves that are blue-green, hairless, finely divided, and all basal. The large 4-petaled flowers (March–May) readily drop their petals when disturbed, such as on a windy day. Fruits are an elongated capsule (dry fruit full of seeds). The road to Willow Beach is a good place to see fields of Desert gold poppy mixed with fields of Suncups in wet spring seasons.

LITTLE GOLD POPPY

Eschscholtzia minutiflora S. Watson
Poppy Family (Papaveraceae)

Little gold poppy is a small but showy annual that is about half the size of Desert gold poppy. Most plants are smaller than the one pictured. Look for them in rocky places, in washes, and hiding along canyon walls. You might miss this wildflower in spring. Look for the four small, yellow petals that shed easily. *Minutiflora* in Latin means small-flowered. This poppy has one of the smallest flowers of any of our native poppies in the Mojave Desert.

LESSER MOHAVEA
(GOLDEN DESERT SNAPDRAGON)

Antirrhinum mohavea D. J. Keil
(*Mohavea breviflora* Coville)
Plantain Family (Plantaginaceae)

Lesser mohavea is an annual belly plant with sticky glands on its leaves that often trap sand particles. The tubular flowers have distinct maroon spots on the lower petal. Flowers emerge from the axils of the leaves and resemble snapdragon flowers. Turn the flower upside down and it can look like a face with a pair of bulging eyes over an open mouth. This plant is typically found on gravelly slopes near washes and along canyon edges. It was first collected near the Mojave River in California, which explains its name. Recent DNA evidence suggests that this species is properly placed in the genus *Antirrhinum* rather than in *Mohavea*.

DESERT TRUMPET

Eriogonum inflatum Torr. & Frém.
Buckwheat Family (Polygonaceae)

Desert trumpet is a delightful, perennial herb that manages to look quite fragile, yet is surprisingly tough. Its wavy, slender stems have an intriguing growth pattern. Near the end of the long, hollow stems, multiple, thinner flowering stalks grow out in a radial pattern. Most stems feature a dramatic inflated portion just below the radial branches, but because the stems can branch several times, there can be inflations at several places along the stems, before the stems end in smaller flowering branches. The inflation of the stem is a storage organ for gas exchange for photosynthesis. The tiny yellow flowers can appear nearly year-round but are most abundant in spring and autumn, depending on rainfall. In winter, the dried stems often remain standing and turn reddish. Look for this plant along roadsides and washes, and on gravelly slopes throughout the Creosotebush community.

LITTLE DESERT TRUMPET

Eriogonum trichopes Torr.
Buckwheat Family (Polygonaceae)

Little desert trumpet is an annual and a smaller version of its taller relative, Desert trumpet. Little desert trumpet also generally has only one inflated area on the basal stem compared to the possibility of several inflations per stem in Desert trumpet. Little desert trumpet grows across wide swaths of desert, on gravelly slopes and hillsides, and is most discernible when it appears in nearly pure stands. In winter, the dead, reddish stalks remain and give a distinctive fuzzy, brownish hue to the desert slopes, as seen along both Northshore and Temple Bar Roads.

GROUND-CHERRY

Physalis crassifolia Benth.
Nightshade Family (Solanaceae)

The sepals of Ground-cherry flowers inflate and dry into a pocket that encloses the developing, tomato-like fruit. The fruit, unlike many of its close relatives, can be toxic. In fact, most plants in the Nightshade Family have some toxic parts. The petals of the flower are fused together and make a solid yellow "skirt" around the anthers and stigma. Ground-cherry grows in shaded canyons and washes, in rock cracks, and at the base of cliffs.

TRAILING MILKWEED

Funastrum hirtellum (A. Gray) Schltr.
Dogbane Family (Apocynaceae)

Trailing milkweed has beautiful pink to white or cream flowers that grow in umbel-like clusters. The flowers have an interesting mode of pollination: pollen is gathered into packets called pollinia. Instead of the pollen being picked up several grains at a time by insects or birds, as is typical of most flowering plants, the entire pollen packet can stick to a visiting insect's leg and be carried to another plant. Milkweeds are visited by a variety of insects, including butterflies attracted to the abundant nectar. Like most plants in the Dogbane Family, Trailing milkweed produces a toxic milky sap when leaves or stems are broken. It is a perennial, herbaceous vine with short, erect hairs on its stems and is found in washes and canyon edges, often growing in the canopy of host shrubs. Look for large numbers of flowering vines in Grapevine Canyon in March.

MOHAVE THISTLE

Cirsium mohavense (Greene) Petr.
Sunflower Family (Asteraceae)

Mohave thistle has spines everywhere. Only the flowers, which may be white, pink, or lavender, are safe to touch. The flower heads are surrounded by a series of overlapping bracts (phyllaries) that are green and spine-tipped, and the leaves are also spine-tipped, providing protection from herbivores. The flowers are visited by Monarch butterflies on their migration to and from Mexico. The seeds are a favorite food for many songbirds. Mojave thistle is a biennial or perennial herb that is usually found around springs, such as Rogers and Blue Point Springs.

SPANISH NEEDLES

Palafoxia arida B. L. Turner &
M. I. Morris var. *arida*
Sunflower Family (Asteraceae)

The lovely pink disk flowers have light-pink petals and red stamens. The fused stamens form a column in the center through which the stigma emerges. Flowers can be seen March to May but can also be found after autumn rains. The leaves are long, narrow, and somewhat hairy. Spanish needles is named for the long seeds that are topped with stiff awns. This wildflower is frequently found in sandy areas, on dunes, and along roadsides in the Creosotebush community. Look for it on the sand dunes along Fisherman's Trail near Katherine Landing, or in the sandy areas around Willow Beach, and at Redstone.

SALTMARSH FLEABANE

Pluchea odorata (L.) Cass var. *odorata*
Sunflower Family (Asteraceae)

As its common name implies, Saltmarsh flea-bane is found in moist, saline riverbank and marsh habitats. It is also found in the draw-down zone of Lake Mead. This leafy, aromatic herb is typically an annual but can be peren-nial under consistently moist conditions. With its flat-topped heads of pink to magenta disk flowers, Saltmarsh fleabane often stands out among less colorful vegetation. Look for this plant during the summer and early autumn when it flowers.

WIRE LETTUCE

Stephanomeria pauciflora (Torr.) A. Nelson
Sunflower Family (Asteraceae)

Wire lettuce is a delightful small perennial herb that grows in many disturbed places in LMNRA, including along roadsides. The flowers are a simple cluster of five light pink ray flowers. The flower heads can be so tiny that it is possible to miss them. The plant can appear as a tight ball of wiry stems dotted with pink. The seeds have a soft and feathery pappus that promotes wind dispersal to new areas. The stems produce a milky sap similar to the edible lettuce plant, which is also in the Sunflower family.

AFRICAN MUSTARD
Strigosella africana (L.) Botsch.
Mustard Family (Brassicaceae)

African mustard is a nonnative annual that has naturalized in LMNRA. It is an upright branched herb with hairy stems and leaves. Pink-violet flowers conform to the typical mustard configuration of four petals, six stamens, and an ovary that sits above the petals and sepals. The fruit is an elongated pod (silique) that grows nearly perpendicular to the stem. African mustard colonizes disturbed areas, abandoned fields, roadsides, and the drawdown zone of Boulder Basin. Massive quantities of this plant are found on the trail to the St. Thomas ghost town.

TUMBLEWEED (RUSSIAN THISTLE)
Salsola tragus L.
Goosefoot Family (Chenopodiaceae)

Tumbleweed has become a symbol of the arid West, rolling across the dry landscape and stacking up against fences. It is, however, not native to the United States but was brought here in bales of contaminated flax seed from Russia in the 1870s. Tumbleweed is a prickly annual that branches profusely from its base with longitudinally ribbed stems that are generally red striped. It can grow up to 3 feet tall in LMNRA and has a hemispherical shape. Leaves are spine-tipped and the flowers are white to pink. After the plant starts to die, the top of the plant can break off from the root and tumble across the landscape in the wind, spreading seeds as it goes. Tumbleweed is now found in every state in the United States.

ARIZONA LUPINE
Lupinus arizonicus (S. Watson) S. Watson
Legume Family (Fabaceae)

Arizona lupine is the most common of the six species of lupine in LMNRA. This wildflower is an erect, branched annual, with palmately compound leaves. The light pink to magenta, pea-like flowers can be seen March to May in sandy washes, along roadsides, and on gravel slopes in the Creosotebush community. Look for large displays in good wildflower years along the road to Willow Beach and in Grapevine Canyon.

FILAREE
(CRANESBILL, REDSTEM FILAREE)
Erodium cicutarium (L.) L'Hér ex Aiton
Geranium Family (Geraniaceae)

Filaree is an introduced, nonnative species from Eurasia and is found in every state of the United States. It is widespread in the Creosotebush community throughout LMNRA. Filaree was apparently introduced as early as the 1700s into Southern California, based on pollen and plant parts found in mud layers in bricks used in building Spanish missions. The leaves are highly divided and spread along the ground surface. The tiny magenta flowers open only in the morning and drop their petals by afternoon. The fruits are pointed and sit upright, resembling a crane's or stork's bill. The seeds of this plant have an unusual method of dispersal: the seed can drill itself into the soil. It does this using a long tail (awn), which coils and uncoils based on the changing amount of moisture in the environment.

WEAKSTEM MARIPOSA
Calochortus flexuosus S. Watson
Lily Family (Liliaceae)

DESERT FIVESPOT
Eremalche rotundifolia (A. Gray) Greene
Mallow Family (Malvaceae)

Although uncommonly seen in the LMNRA, Weakstem mariposa is quite conspicuous when it flowers. The bulb was once a food source for Native Americans. This wildflower is a perennial with a trailing, sinuous, vine-like stem. It typically grows with the support of nearby shrubs. The leaves are small, basal, and short-lived. The flowers (April to May) are erect and bell-shaped, with lilac-colored petals that have purple spots and a yellow interior. Look for this wildflower on rocky soils and desert pavement in good wildflower years in the Creosotebush community. Photo by Kathlyn Powell.

You will be lucky to find this little gem of a plant. Desert fivespot appears in rocky areas of the Creosotebush community during years with sufficient rainfall. The round leaves have scalloped edges and are sparsely covered with hairs in star-shaped clusters. The flowers (March to May) have five light-purple petals forming a cupped globe. Each petal has a distinctive red or dark purple spot, like a red flame, on its inner base. The fruit is a papery capsule with individual black seeds stacked together like casino chips.

PURPLE MAT

Nama demissa A. Gray
Nama Family (Namaceae) or
Borage Family (Boraginaceae)

Purple mat is a ground-hugging annual belly plant with forked, hairy stems and spoon-shaped leaves. In the axils of the leaves, tubular, magenta flowers (March to May) grow singly and have yellow stamens. Many plants grow together, forming mats of color against the tan desert landscape. Purple mat thrives in desert washes and gravelly areas in the Creosotebush community.

SAND VERBENA

Abronia villosa S. Watson var. *villosa*
Four O'Clock Family (Nyctaginaceae)

As the name suggests, Sand verbena is found on sand dunes and in other places with sandy soils. The inflorescence is composed of clusters of trumpet-shaped flowers that emit a delicate odor, particularly at dawn or dusk. The many sticky hairs on the leaves typically result in a coating of sand grains. Look for this wildflower at Sandy Cove in good wildflower years. Photo by Kathlyn Powell.

GIANT FOUR O'CLOCK

Mirabilis multiflora (Torr.) A.Gray
Four O'Clock Family (Nyctaginaceae)

The scientific name means beautiful multiflow-
ered plant, in reference to its many flowers aris-
ing from a single floral cup. The common name
refers to the flowers that open in late afternoon and wither by the following morning.
The five-part, magenta-colored flowers (April
to September) are funnel shaped and produce
a smooth, dark-brown fruit. The stamens and
stigma stick out beyond the edge of the fused
petals. A mature plant can have hundreds of
flowers blooming simultaneously. Look for
Giant four o'clock in well-drained, sandy soils
and along Christmas Tree Pass.

DESERT PAINTBRUSH

Castilleja chromosa A. Nelson
Broomrape Family (Orobanchaceae)

Desert paintbrush is a root parasite. It has special structures that allow it to tap into the roots
of nearby shrubs, thereby "stealing" water
and nutrients. This strategy provides access
to moisture even in the driest months of the
year. Desert paintbrush grows on rocky slopes
and often adds a colorful punctuation to the
gray-green foliage in Joshua tree and Pinyon
pine-Juniper communities. This perennial herb
grows from a woody crown each year with
hairy stems and narrow, lobed leaves. What
we see as red petals (April to July) are actually
red-tipped bracts that surround and protect the
smaller flowers within. Look for this plant in the
Newberry Mountains.

DESERT MONKEYFLOWER

Diplacus bigelovii (A. Gray) G. L. Nesom
(*Mimulus bigelovii* (A. Gray) A. Gray)
Lopseed Family (Phyrmaceae)

One of the most delightful sights in a good wildflower spring is of the masses of magenta Desert monkeyflowers decorating gravelly or sandy washes in the Creosotebush community. These glandular-haired, annual plants can be so small as to qualify as belly plants, and the flowers are so wonderfully large and conspicuous that you might wonder how they are held up. The flowers can be two to three times larger than the leaves. Enjoy your fill of these wildflowers, as they flower for only a short time from March to April. Look for fields of these flowers in gravelly washes at Grapevine Canyon, Jumbo Wash, and Bonelli Wash.

PALMER'S PENSTEMON (BEARDTONGUE)

Penstemon palmeri A. Gray
Plantain Family (Plantaginaceae)

Palmer's penstemon has five stamens, one of which is sterile and modified with long, beard-like yellow hairs, giving rise to the alternate common name of Beardtongue. Bees and birds, including hummingbirds, pollinate the elegant, pink flowers. This upright perennial herb has hairless, whitish stems and grayish-green, fleshy leaves with toothed margins. The leaves diminish in size upward along the stem and come in pairs. The upper, paired leaves are fused together around the stem. This wildflower often grows on the edge of washes and roadsides.

ROCK GILIA

Gilia scopulorum M. E. Jones
Phlox Family (Polemoniaceae)

Rock gilia is a tiny, annual wildflower that requires you to look for it on rocky and gravelly areas and on desert pavement in the Creosotebush community. There are five species of *Gilia* in LMNRA, but this one is the most common and most likely to be seen. *Gilia* species readily hybridize, making identification difficult. Look for a tuft of finely divided leaves at the base of a short flowering stalk. Each stalk has a branch tipped with a tubular pink flower that has a yellow throat and blue pollen. The sepals are dotted with glands that may be sticky to touch. As you adventure in LMNRA, you will be pleased to find this little beauty.

DESERT ASTER

Xylorhiza tortifolia (Torr. &
A. Gray) Greene var. *tortifolia*
Sunflower Family (Asteraceae)

Desert aster is a lovely, perennial subshrub that is always a treat to find in the field in March and April. The soft pink to light-violet ray flowers contrast with the bright yellow center of disk flowers. It grows in many places in LMNRA, particularly along Northshore Road near Northshore Summit Trail and on the edges of gypsum outcrops in the Creosotebush community. The leaves of this wildflower are light green and have spine-tipped lobes.

MOJAVE LUPINE (COULTER'S LUPINE)

Lupinus sparsiflorus Benth.
Legume Family (Fabaceae)

If you love large blue wildflower displays, the Mojave lupine does not disappoint. It is common in wet springs, particularly along roadsides and in sandy washes on the Arizona side of the Colorado River; along roads toward Katherine Landing, near Grapevine Spring; and along the road to Willow Beach. Mojave lupine can grow in dense patches when rainfall is sufficient. As with other lupines, it moves its leaves during the day to face the sun. Roots of many lupines contain nitrogen-fixing bacteria that may enrich the soil for the lupine. Arizona lupine is very similar, but the flowers are pink.

NOTCHLEAF PHACELIA (SCORPIONWEED)

Phacelia crenulata S. Watson
Waterleaf Family (Hydrophyllaceae)
or Borage Family (Boraginaceae)

Notchleaf phacelia is one of the most common deep blue to purple wildflowers in the Creosotebush community in March and April. There are fifteen recorded species in this genus in LMNRA, many of them occurring in rocky communities or on desert pavement. Do not attempt to touch these plants: The glands on the leaves of the phacelias can cause a contact dermatitis for some people. The flowers grow in a type of inflorescence called a cyme. The inflorescence in this species is coiled, like the tail of a scorpion. Notchleaf refers to the deeply lobed leaves of the plant. Look for Notchleaf phacelia in wet spring seasons along roadsides, particularly Lakeshore Road, and in the lower part of Christmas Tree Pass. Also look for an abundance of this wildflower in Jumbo Wash and along the road to Willow Beach. Photo by Kathlyn Powell.

COMMON PHACELIA

Phacelia distans Benth.
Waterleaf Family (Hydrophyllaceae)
or Borage Family (Boraginaceae)

Common phacelia can be distinguished from Notchleaf phacelia and other LMNRA phacelias by its sky-blue to violet flowers and its habit of growing beneath shrubs in the Creosotebush community. *Phacelia* comes from the Greek meaning bundled, and *distans* meaning widely spaced, in reference to its stamens. This lovely straggling plant can be found in Bonelli Wash in the spring. Also look for it under shrubs along Temple Bar Road.

YELLOWTHROATS (FREMONT'S PHACELIA)

Phacelia fremontii Torr.
Waterleaf Family (Hydrophyllaceae)
or Borage Family (Boraginaceae)

Yellowthroats can be identified by its pink to lavender tubular flowers with yellow throats. Because the leaves are covered with sticky hairs, they often collect sand grains on their surfaces and can reflect sunlight, thereby cooling the leaves and reducing water loss. However, like the other phacelias, this one can also cause contact dermatitis. The flowers have a strong skunk smell and vary in color from lavender to violet. Native bees are particularly attracted to this plant.

PALMER'S PHACELIA

Phacelia palmeri Torr. ex S. Watson
Waterleaf Family (Hydrophyllaceae)
or Borage Family (Boraginaceae)

Palmer's phacelia is found on gypsum soils, particularly along Northshore Road and near Rogers Spring in LMNRA. This phacelia is also remarkable because it is a biennial, that is, it grows as a rosette for the first year of life and then sends up a large flowering stalk and sets seed in its second spring and then dies. The light blue to white flowers (April to May) are almost hidden under the sticky, foul-smelling, gland-dotted leaves and can even appear closed. The overall appearance of the plant is of a narrow, triangular cone, wide at the base then tapering upward. Insects that are attracted to the flowers can get stuck on the leaves of this plant.

CHIA

Salvia columbariae Benth.
Mint Family (Lamiaceae)

Chia is the most common annual wildflower of the Mint family and can easily be found in many places of LMNRA. Look for green, upright stems with balls of blue flowers. The bracts of the flower clusters can be purple. The leaves grow mostly near the ground and are ruffled. The whorled arrangement of flowers on the stems is typical of many plants in the Mint family. The tiny seeds have an outer layer that absorbs water and forms a mucilaginous mass when wet. The seeds were eaten in the past by Native Americans. Today, the seeds of a related plant (*Salvia hispanica*) are sold as a high-protein, high-fiber food. A good place to find this wildflower is in Grapevine Canyon. The other two *Salvias* in LMNRA, Desert Sage and Mohave Sage, are both shrubs. Photo by Kathlyn Powell.

BRISTLY GILIA
(BRISTLY LANGLOISIA)

Langloisia setosissima (Torr. &
A. Gray) Greene subsp. *setosissima*
Phlox Family (Polemoniaceae)

Bristly gilia is a belly plant that grows in small, circular tufts. The leaves have stiff bristles at the edges of their three to five lobes. The flowers (March to May) have light-purple petals. The fruit has a triangular shape in cross-section and the seeds become gelatinous when wet. Bristly gilia can be quite abundant and, where present, adds a bright color to sandy or rocky flats. The related Lilac sunbonnet (*Langloisia setosissima* subsp. *punctata*), also in LMNRA, has lighter-colored petals punctuated with dark dots. Look for these plants on desert pavement in the Creosotebush community.

DESERT LARKSPUR
(MOJAVE LARKSPUR)

Delphinium parishii A. Gray subsp. *parishii*
Buttercup Family (Ranunculaceae)

Desert larkspur is a perennial plant that dies back to the root at the end of flowering. Plants may not even show up in dry years. The name *Delphinium* (Greek for "dolphin") refers to the unopened flower buds that look like tiny dolphins. Look carefully in sandy, gravelly, and rocky crevices and on desert pavement for this lovely wildflower.

PIGWEED AMARANTH (TUMBLE PIGWEED)

Amaranthus albus L.
Amaranth Family (Amaranthaceae)

This nonnative annual plant looks superficially like Tumbleweed (*Salsola tragus*) and can grow in the same habitat: disturbed, weedy places from which native vegetation has been removed or damaged. Plants usually grow in an upright form like a tumbleweed. Flowers are small, and both male and female flowers occur together in spiny clusters. It is called Pigweed because the plants were supposedly fed to pigs. This plant is found in all US states and in Europe and Australia. Look for this plant almost exclusively along the drawdown zone of Lake Mead; it is especially common at Boulder Beach.

HONEYSWEET

Tidestromia suffruticosa (Torr.)
Standl. var. *oblongifolia* (S. Watson)
Sánch.Pino & Flores Olv.
Amaranth Family (Amaranthaceae)

Honeysweet has the remarkable ability to grow in the heat of the summer when most other plants are dormant. It has a different photosynthetic system from most of the other Mojave Desert wildflowers that allows it to thrive in high heat. Although you may find this plant as a belly plant in some areas of LMNRA, in certain areas, such as near Rogers Spring, and along roadsides, where water is sometimes abundant, Honeysweet can become a rather large and conspicuous shrub. The lovely little flowers of this plant are so small you are likely to miss them, which is why we put this plant in our inconspicuous category.

COCKLEBUR

Xanthium strumarium L.
Sunflower Family (Asteraceae)

Cocklebur is a nonnative, invasive plant in LMNRA that has invaded along Las Vegas Wash and the Lake Mead shoreline in the Government Wash area. Flowers (July to October) are all disk flowers with the tiny male flowers clustered at the top of the stem and the larger, but fewer, female flowers in the leaf axils. Both flowers are relatively inconspicuous. Female flowers, however, develop into a conspicuous fruit, a bur, with stiffly hooked bristles. Each fruit has two seeds, usually one larger than the other. The hooked fruits are readily dispersed because they cling to the fur and skin of animals and to human clothes and also float in water. The burs of this plant were the inspiration for the invention of Velcro.

PEPPERGRASS

Lepidium lasiocarpum Nutt.
subsp. *lasiocarpum*
Mustard Family (Brassicaceae)

Peppergrass is not a grass but a tiny plant in the Mustard family. The common name comes from the smell and sharp taste of pepper. Peppergrass is one of the first wildflowers to emerge after winter rains and can flower, go to seed, and die even before other wildflowers make their appearance in spring. *Lepidium* comes from the Greek *lepidion* (little scale) in reference to its flattened seed pod. Peppergrass can be found in many places in LMNRA in rocky or sandy washes or on rocky flats.

CALIFORNIA DODDER
(CHAPARRAL DODDER)

Cuscuta californica Hook. & Arn.
Morning-Glory Family (Convolvulaceae)

California dodder is also sometimes called Witches' hair because it appears as a tangle of thin orange stems that wind around shrubs in the spring. The plant is parasitic on its shrub hosts. Although California dodder germinates from seeds in the soil, the stems find their way to a shrub and attach to the stems of the shrub by haustoria, which are root-like connections that suck water and nutrients from the host plant. Most shrubs can survive this parasite, but some smaller shrubs may eventually die. The small, clustered, creamy white, bell-shaped flowers appear from May to August. Look for California dodder along roadsides in most areas of LMNRA.

WOOLLY PLANTAIN

Plantago ovata Forssk.
Plantain Family (Plantaginaceae)

Woolly plantain looks like a grass due to its long leaves and compact flower head, but it actually has tiny papery flowers, totally unlike the flowers of grasses. It is common in spring almost anywhere in LMNRA and can sometimes cover the ground. Woolly plantain is a part of the diet of the Desert tortoise (*Gopherus agassizii*).

BRITTLE SPINEFLOWER

Chorizanthe brevicornu Torr. var. *brevicornu*
Buckwheat Family (Polygonaceae)

Brittle spineflower is a small erect annual with a forked branching pattern. It can have reddish lower leaves and stems and yellow-green upper stems. Brittle spineflower is common throughout the Creosotebush community in LMNRA. Look for this plant in rocky, gravelly areas and on desert pavement.

SPINY HERB (DEVIL'S SPINEFLOWER)

Chorizanthe rigida (Torr.) Torr. & A. Gray
Buckwheat Family (Polygonaceae)

Do not sit down on Spiny herb! The plant is only green in the spring. During the rest of the year, this tiny wildflower looks like a reddish, miniature cactus. The leaves are spine-tipped and when dry can be painful to touch. The flowers of this plant are so small that they seem almost microscopic. Look for Spiny herb on rocky slopes and desert pavement.

DESERT MISTLETOE

Phoradendron californicum Nutt.
Mistletoe Family (Viscaceae)

Desert mistletoe is considered an aerial, semiparasite because it grows in the branches of trees and shrubs, taking water and nutrients from the host plant, but is also capable of photosynthesis. The mature mistletoe berries are sought by Phainopepla birds, and these birds spread the undigested, sticky seeds from tree to tree while feeding on the fruits. *Phoradendron* is Greek for tree thief, referring to its parasitic habit. Desert mistletoe grows mostly on leguminous plants, especially branches of Paloverde, Honey and Screwbean mesquite, and Catclaw, but also occasionally on Creosotebush. The bright red, pink, and yellow berries are conspicuous in late spring.

Flower Color Cross-Reference Guide

This list provides reference by flower color to plants not included in the Wildflower section.

White and Cream Flowers

Trees: Goodding's black willow, Catclaw

Shrubs: Rush milkweed, Cheesebush, Seepwillow, Desert baccharis, Arrowleaf, Desert alyssum, Thurber's sandpaper plant, Desert buckwheat, Desert almond, Box-thorn

Yuccas: Beargrass, Banana yucca, Joshua tree, Mojave yucca

Yellow and Orange Flowers

Trees: Paloverde, Western honey mesquite, Tree tobacco

Shrubs: Chaffbush, Parish's goldeneye, Sweetbush, Brittlebush, Virgin River brittlebush, Sticky snakeweed, Pygmy cedar, Paperflower, Mojave cottonthorn, Spiny goldenbush, Nevada ephedra, Torrey ephedra, Sand croton, Bush trefoil, Spiny senna, Globemallow, Blackbrush, Creosotebush

Cacti: Buckhorn cholla, Cottontop cactus, Barrel cactus, Devil cholla, Grizzly bear prickly pear

Red, Pink, and Magenta Flowers

Trees: Desert willow, Athel

Shrubs: Arrowweed, Ocotillo, Pima rhatany, Desert buckwheat, Saltcedar

Cacti: Hedgehog cactus, Fishhook cactus, Beavertail, Pygmy barrel cactus

Blue and Purple Flowers

Trees: Smoketree

Shrubs: Indigobush, Desert lavender, Desert Sage, Bladdersage, Desert rue

Inconspicuous Flowers

Trees: California juniper, Turbinella oak, Singleleaf pinyon pine, Fremont cottonwood

Shrubs: White bursage, Woolly bursage, Four-wing saltbush, Desert holly, Lenscale, Winterfat, Sand croton, Canyon grape

Sedges and Grasses: Most sedge and grass flowers are inconspicuous

Plant Structures

LEAF SHAPES

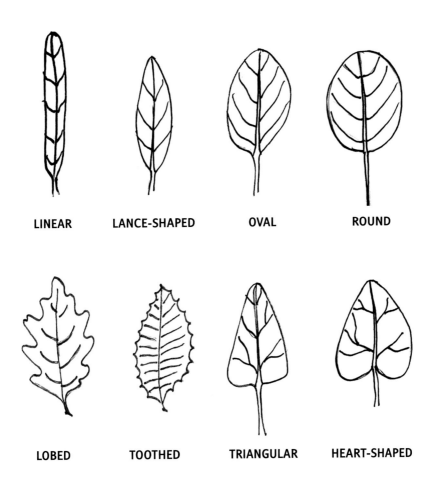

LINEAR   LANCE-SHAPED   OVAL   ROUND

LOBED   TOOTHED   TRIANGULAR   HEART-SHAPED

LEAF ARRANGEMENTS

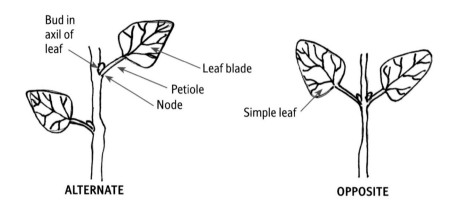

Bud in axil of leaf

Leaf blade

Petiole

Node

ALTERNATE

Simple leaf

OPPOSITE

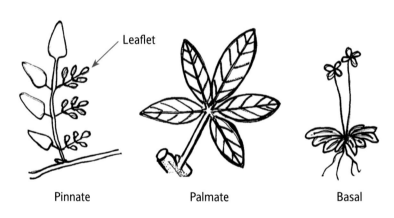

Leaflet

Pinnate   Palmate   Basal

COMPOUND LEAVES

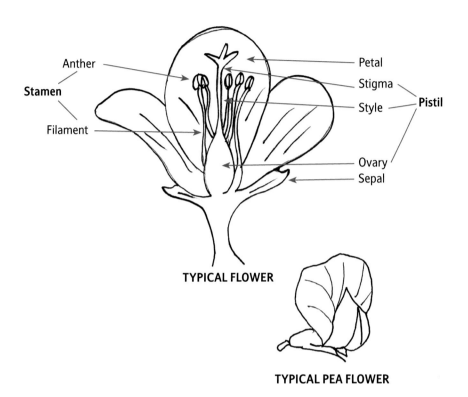

Stamen
Anther
Filament

Petal
Stigma
Style
Ovary
Sepal

Pistil

TYPICAL FLOWER

TYPICAL PEA FLOWER

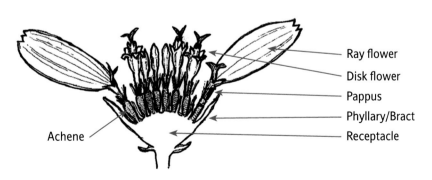

Ray flower
Disk flower
Pappus
Phyllary/Bract
Receptacle

Achene

TYPICAL SUNFLOWER

INFLORESCENCE TYPES

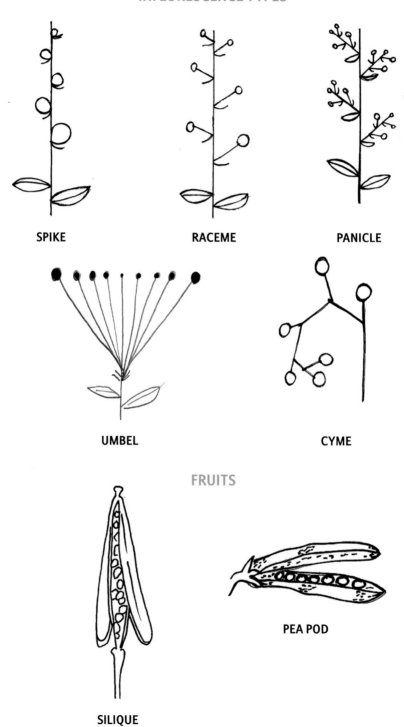

SPIKE

RACEME

PANICLE

UMBEL

CYME

FRUITS

SILIQUE

PEA POD

Glossary

Starred terms (*) are illustrated in the plant structures section.

*achene. A small, dry, one-seeded fruit of plants in the Sunflower or Buckwheat family.

*alternate leaf. A leaf borne singly at each node on a stem (contrast with opposite leaf).

annual. A plant that completes its life cycle within a single year (contrast with biennial, perennial).

*anther. The part of the stamen that produces pollen.

awn. An elongated bristle-like appendage that can occur on a plant structure, often found on the seeds of grasses.

*axil. The location between a stem and a leaf base where flower and branch buds arise.

belly plant. A short or tiny plant best observed by bending over or laying on one's belly.

biennial. A plant that completes its life cycle within two years, producing vegetative growth the first year, and flowering the second year.

*bract. A reduced leaf-like structure that can mimic a petal, sepal, leaf, or other plant part.

*bud. An unexpanded leaf, shoot, or flower. Buds can be found in axils of leaves or at the growing end of shoots or stems.

bunchgrass. A perennial grass that grows in discrete tufts or clumps, as distinct from sod-like grass.

calyx. The outer whorl of a flower; the collective term for all the sepals (usually green) of the flower (see sepal).

catkin. A spike inflorescence consisting of a dense cluster of flowers of the same sex; found on plants in the Willow family (see spike).

*compound leaf. A whole leaf separated into two or more distinct and identical parts called leaflets (see palmate leaf, pinnate leaf, contrast with simple leaf).

*cyme. A coiled, flat-topped, rounded, or branched inflorescence in which the outermost, or uppermost flower blooms first.

deciduous. Loss of leaves in winter and/or during summer droughts (contrast with evergreen).

desert pavement. A rocky, smooth surface formed from erosion and removal of small rocks and sand.

dioecious. Having male and female flowers on separate plants of the same species (contrast with monoecious).

*disk flower. The central flowers in an inflorescence of some members of the Sunflower family; disk flowers can appear along with ray flowers or by themselves in a flower head (contrast with ray flower).

evergreen. Retaining leaves throughout the year (contrast with deciduous).

family. A botanical ranking that includes a group of genera resembling one another in general and technical characteristics (see genus, species, variety).

*filament. A thread-like stalk of the stamen supporting the pollen-bearing anther (see stamen).

flower head. A dense clustering of flowers; an inflorescence that is often mistaken for a single flower such as in the Sunflower family.

fruit. The mature ovary with its enclosed seed(s); fruits can be fleshy or dry.

genus (plural: genera). A botanical ranking comprising one or more similar species; the genus is the first word in a plant's scientific name, followed by the species name.

glochid. A barbed hair, bristle, or fine spine found especially on species of *Opuntia* in the Cactus family.

inflorescence. The arrangement of flowers on a floral axis; a cluster of flowers.

*leaflet. A leaf-like division of a compound leaf.

monoecious. Having separate male and female flowers on the same plant (contrast with dioecious).

*node. The position on the stem where leaves and branches originate.

*opposite leaf. A leaf borne across from another leaf at the same node (contrast with alternate leaf).

*ovary. The expanded basal portion of the pistil (female part of the flower) that contains the developing seeds.

*palmate leaf. Lobed, veined, or divided from a common point like the fingers of the hand.

*panicle. A branched inflorescence with flowers maturing from the bottom up.

pappus. A modified group of hairs or membranous structures at the apex of achenes in the Sunflower family.

parasite. An organism that obtains its food or water from a host organism.

*pea flower. A flower in which all petals are not similar in size and arrangement, often appearing two-lipped.

*petiole. The part of a leaf that is the leaf stalk or stem that attaches a leaf blade to the stem of a plant.

perennial. A plant that lives for several or many years.

*petal. A single segment of the flower that sits just inside the sepals (calyx) and is usually colorful.

photosynthesis. A process by which green plants convert carbon dioxide and water into carbohydrates in the presence of sunlight.

*phyllary. A bract enclosing or under the flower heads in the Sunflower family; their arrangement, number, color, shape, and size are useful for identification.

*pinnate leaf. A compound leaf that has separate leaflets that grow along each side of an axis; feather-like.

*pistil. The female structure of a flower, typically consisting of an ovary, style, and stigma.

prickle. A sharp-pointed outgrowth from epidermal tissues of the stem, such as with roses or Catclaw (contrast with spine, thorn).

*raceme. An elongated, unbranched inflorescence of flowers with flower stalks, maturing from the bottom upward.

*ray flower. One of the outer flowers in a flower head of some plants in the Sunflower family. Ray flowers have a single obvious petal and can occur with disk flowers or alone in a flower head (contrast with disk flower).

*receptacle. A platform at the end of the flowering stem that bears the flower parts; especially evident in plants of the Sunflower family.

rhizome. A root-like, underground stem that has buds, shoots, and roots.

scale. A membranous leaf-like structure.

*sepal. A single segment of the calyx.

*silique. An elongated, pod-like fruit with a central membrane; in the Mustard family.

*simple leaf. An undivided leaf blade that is not separated into leaflets, although it may have a lobed margin (contrast with compound leaf)

species (plural: species). A taxonomic grouping of closely related, mutually fertile individuals; the basic unit of classification (see genus); in a scientific name, the species name always follows the name of the genus.

*spike. An unbranched, elongated, and usually dense cluster of flowers directly attached to the flowering stalk, maturing from the bottom upward.

spikelet. The basic flower cluster unit of grasses and sedges, consisting of one to many flowers subtended by two bracts at its base.

spine. A sharp-pointed, woody outgrowth, derived from leaf tissue; obvious on Date palm, Ocotillo, and most cacti (contrast with prickle, thorn).

*stamen. Male sex organ usually consisting of an anther and filament.

*stigma. The often-sticky portion of the female flower receptive to pollen at the top of the style.

*style. The elongated portion of the female flower that holds the stigma aloft.

subshrub. A plant that has woody, perennial lower or basal stems and nonwoody, upper stems that may die back annually.

subspecies (subsp.). A taxonomic category immediately below species, with consistent traits different from the parent species, like color or distribution, but not sufficiently distinct to be considered its own species.

*sunflower. A cluster of flowers in the Sunflower family with ray and/or disk flowers plus pappus, achenes, a receptacle, and bracts (phyllaries).

synonym. In botany, a previous but still occasionally used name for a species, genus, or family.

tendril. A twining, thread-like, specialized leaf that enables a plant to secure support.

thorn. A modified, sharp-pointed stem, occurring in the axil of a leaf where a branch would normally develop, such as the thorns of Western honey mesquite (contrast with prickle, spine).

*umbel. An inflorescence in which three to many flower stalks radiate from a common point.

variety (var.). A taxonomic category below that of species or subspecies with a frequently variable trait such as flower color or habit (see family, genus, species).

Suggested Reading

Baldwin, B. G., D. H. Goldman, D. J. Keil, R. Patterson, T. J. Rosatti, and D. J. Wilken, eds. *The Jepson Manual: Vascular Plants of California, 2nd edition*. Oakland: University of California Press, 2012.

Charlet, D. A. *Nevada Mountains: Landforms, Trees, and Vegetation.* Salt Lake City: University of Utah Press, 2020.

Clinesmith, Larry L., and Elsie L. Sellars. *Red Rock Canyon Plants.* Tehachapi, CA: Red Rock Canyon Interpretive Association, 2001.

Foster, J. *Lake Mead National Recreation Area: A History of America's First National Playground.* Reno: University of Nevada Press, 2016.

Holland, James S. 1978. *Flowering Plants of the Lake Mead Region.* Popular Series 22. Tucson: Southwest Parks and Monument Association, 1978.

Holland, J. S., W. E. Niles, and P. J. Leary. *Vascular Plants of the Lake Mead National Recreation Area.* Lake Mead Technical Report 3, 1979.

Jepson Flora Project Jepson-eFlora, https://ucjeps.berkeley.edu/eflora/, 2022.

MacKay, P. 2013. *Mojave Desert Wildflowers, 2nd ed.* Helena, MT: Falcon Guide, 2013.

Moulin, T. *Red Rock Canyon Visitor Guide.* Snell Press, 2013.

Spellenberg, R. *North American Wildflowers: Western Region.* New York: Knopf, 2001.

Stewart, J. M. *Mojave Desert Wildflowers.* Albuquerque, NM: Jon Stewart Photography, 1998.

Walker, L. W., and F. H. Landau. *A Natural History of the Mojave Desert.* Tucson: University of Arizona, 2018.

Western National Parks Association. *Lake Mead National Recreation Area Plants, Cacti and Shrubs.* Tampa, FL: Waterford Press, 2016.

Western National Parks Association. *Wildflowers of Lake Mead National Recreation Area.* Tampa, FL: Waterford Press, 2016.

Index

About the Authors

Elizabeth A. Powell has an MS in biology and a PhD in botany. She has published a number of scientific papers on pollination ecology and conservation biology, taught biology and ecology at the University of Puerto Rico, worked as a science editor for the US Geological Survey, and worked as a crew leader for the Bureau of Land Management. As the botanist at Lake Mead National Recreation Area (1996–2005), Powell managed rare and invasive plants.

Frederick H. Landau was a research associate at the University of Nevada Las Vegas (UNLV) where he conducted research on plant ecology and plant physiology and taught courses in plant taxonomy, economic botany, and field ecology. He has published a number of scientific papers and coauthored a book entitled *A Natural History of the Mojave Desert* with Walker.

Lawrence R. Walker has an MS in botany and a PhD in plant ecology. He has published over 140 scientific papers and eleven books, including the one noted above with Landau. Walker retired from teaching ecology, conservation biology, and scientific writing at UNLV in 2018 but continues writing and exploring the Mojave Desert and environs. His most recent book is entitled *Comparative Plant Succession among Terrestrial Biomes of the World*.